Holy Ground

Cathedrals in the Twenty-First Century

— EDITED BY —

STEPHEN PLATTEN

Sacristy
Press

Sacristy Press
PO Box 612, Durham, DH1 9HT

www.sacristy.co.uk

First published in 2017 by Sacristy Press, Durham

Sacristy Limited, registered in England & Wales, number 7565667

British Library Cataloguing-in-Publication Data
A catalogue record for the book is available from the British Library

Paperback ISBN 978-1-910519-73-8
Hardback ISBN 978-1-910519-76-9

FOREWORD

Frank Field

Christianity may die out in this country. Lord Carey, Archbishop of Canterbury from 1991 to 2002, believes this to be a distinct possibility. And maybe it is God's will that this should happen. The chances of this occurring, however, are greatly increased if we simply leave the future to the Spirit and hope for the best.

An alternative approach, and one which I favour, is to throw ourselves into the task of preventing the Carey scenario from becoming true. At least four lines of advance are open to us.

The first depends on the way we live our personal lives as Christians. William Temple, ever anxious to play a key part in changing the world around us, and thereby advancing the kingdom of God, advocated a political programme and did so for practically the whole of his life. But Temple admitted that most political change would come about by Christians living out their lives as an example of the kingdom, both advancing its domain and attracting followers thereby, and that this Christian body should be active in politics in deciding who gets what, when, and how.

A second defence against the annihilation of Christianity in this country as we have known it comes from the present Archbishop of Canterbury, Justin Welby. Justin needed no reminding from his predecessor how precarious is the hold of Christianity on the public consciousness of England. Hence the £24 million a year for ten years that the Church Commissioners made available to Justin to develop areas of growth in those parishes most likely to bear fruit from this investment.

Government has presented the Church with a third and God-given strategy to prevent the dying out of Christianity in this country, and with no extra cost to the Church. This comes in the form of the free school strategy. The Conservative government looks like being in power long enough to change irreversibly the face of English education. It is pursuing this goal, first, by destroying English local government. From being distinct centres of power, separate from central government, local authorities will be at best reduced to commissioning agents. Such are the budget cuts they are suffering and will continue to suffer for the foreseeable future. Hand in hand with this policy is one of converting schools to academy status and catering for the new demand for school places by allowing only free schools to fill the gap.

The Conservatives pledged in 2015 that the government would establish 500 free schools by 2020 and the Church of England has responded by declaring its aim of bagging 125 of this total. Here is a wonderful example of the Church picking up the ball and running with it. For this free school programme presents the Church with its last big opportunity to extend its influence in English education. How cathedrals could have a role in adding to the number of church schools is a subject to which I shall return.

A fourth strategy to prevent the loss of a Christian presence in England comes from the role that English cathedrals have found themselves promoting. Increasing knowledge of the range of their work and the scope of their activities is one of the purposes of this volume. I wish to add to this aim by writing of the politics of the cathedral's role in maintaining knowledge about Christianity. We have already reached the stage where Christian language is a barrier to, rather than a purveyor of, meaning for the majority of English citizens. The figures the national Church publishes regularly echo the danger of England becoming a desert with respect to Anglicanism. The key indicators are Christmas and Easter communicants, baptismal figures, weddings, and funerals. They all point in the same direction.

Contrast this dismal record with what is happening in English cathedrals. In stark contrast to this near-catastrophic decline, the numbers attending cathedral services are on the up, as is the number of visitors. Not by great amounts if we come to services, I grant you, but cathedrals are bucking every other trend we know about allegiance to the Anglican Church.

How might this trend be advanced? Let me deal with two activities I have been and am involved with, both of which were and are aimed at cathedral growth. The first was my chairmanship of the Cathedrals Fabric Commission for England (CFCE). The Commission is the planning authority for the 42 Anglican cathedrals (except for Sodor and Man and Christ Church, Oxford). Any cathedral wishing to change its fabric permanently needs to gain the permission of the Commission. Over the last ten years the Commission has changed from an essentially conservation blocking body to a near revolutionary one, enhancing and encouraging cathedral growth.

When I became chair in 2005, Church House was a pretty cautious body. However, there was an appetite for change amongst the Commissioners, and the staff were encouraged to move from a position of having a near breakdown if a cathedral asked permission to rid itself of a few pews, to supporting a Commission which encouraged and then approved for Chapter a development of the scale of the cloister at Blackburn. This latter development is both marvellous in itself, as it is the first to be built as an addition to the cathedral since the Reformation, but also a clear pointer to how the CFCE had transformed itself.

Every other kind of development promoting the role of cathedrals between these two extremes was approved if the Commission believed that the cathedral's role would be advanced in its duties of being a centre of worship and mission, as well as being a protector of the bishop's role in the cathedral, and from the cathedral into the diocese.

The pressure for change on this scale came from a number of sources apart from the CFCE's commissioners being open for business for such developments. Some deans were natural reformers, wisely wishing to see the civic and spiritual influence of their cathedral on public life increase. Encouraging this stimulus was the establishment of the National Lottery, part of whose funds went to enhancing and adding to England's historic fabric. Big money became available for deans to think big.

But at first, all too many deans saw the Commission as a bulwark against any really imaginative development. I was brought up sharp on how deans saw the CFCE's restrictive role very early on in my stewardship. I was part of a CFCE delegation to Southwark Cathedral so that we might better understand the requests made in its then-current application to the Commission.

I was resting against the first main column, viewing the Victorian development of the nave, when a conversation was struck up between the then Dean, Colin Slee, and the cathedral's extraordinarily talented architect, Richard Griffiths, on the other side of the column. In a voice that was pitched to reach Lichfield without the help of modern technology, Colin exclaimed that he had maximized what he could ever expect the Commission to approve.

I then reappeared around the column to request that Colin should not second-guess the Commission. Deans must tell the Commission what they want to achieve, and should do so on the basis that if one never asks, one never gets. Moreover, telling the Commission openly what deans and chapters wished to achieve over the short and longer run of their stewardship would help develop the Commission's own policy, and particularly in seeing itself as a proactive supporter of the cathedral's role and in the light of what deans and chapters really wished to achieve. That was a message I tried to convey to cathedrals from that point onwards.

Jennie Page's chapter records how the range of the work of the CFCE moved from a negative one, largely concerned with stopping change (in the name of conservation) to the historic fabric, to a proactive one, with the Commission helping cathedrals draw up their plans for advance.

I was concerned with two other major activities during the time I chaired the Commission. The first was to gain additional capital sums. The second aimed at ensuring that the cathedrals could add to the historic role that Elizabeth I had bequeathed, namely cathedral music, and linking this with extending the role of cathedrals in education. Some progress was made on this front. But the sums earmarked for cathedrals by the Wolfson Trust and Pilgrim Trust were small compared to the huge size of the capital needs of English cathedrals. And while governments have been imaginative—thanks to the prompting of cathedrals themselves, the Association of English Cathedrals, and the CFCE—there is no likelihood of any government in the foreseeable future ever finding the resources that cathedrals will need.

Nor will cathedrals raise the sums involved and develop their work as cathedrals if they simply rely on existing fundraising methods. I had hoped that Lambeth Palace would have led a move to try and encourage cathedrals to look to what is mainly the new wealth that has been created in Britain since the Thatcher governments.

A strategic role for Lambeth would be to plan with cathedrals how the new rich, who have capital beyond the dreams of avarice, might be encouraged to take a protective role towards their local cathedral. These new donors need to be given strategic roles in the cathedral, both in its governing structure and in its ceremonial.

Here Westminster Abbey surely leads the way. It has two ancient offices, the High Steward and High Bailiff. The holders of these offices have ceremonial duties within the abbey and get pride of place on feast days, high days and holidays, so to speak. At Westminster, their role is purely ceremonial, but the ceremonial would underscore their value to the cathedral and do so in a clearly recognizable public way. I thought it would be good to think of similar positions in cathedrals so that large donors would be given positions of high rank in cathedral ceremonial in return for the capital they were prepared to invest in the cathedral, and the ongoing advice and stewardship that they would offer to the cathedral chapter. This is clearly unfinished business—even business yet to begin. But if Lambeth is to play a strategic role in ensuring the faith does not die out in this country, a few days' effort on this front could pay huge dividends.

The other concern I had was to protect the Elizabethan tradition of English church music. My first task, once I became chair of the CFCE, was a visit to each of England's Anglican cathedrals. During the visit, I would ask to look at the cathedral's accounts if I had not already seen them online. One thing that stood out clearly for those cathedrals which had choir schools was their huge cost. And while Prime Minister Gordon Brown promised the abolition of boom and bust, I was not so confident, being raised in university at a time when we were taught the power of the trade cycle with its booms and busts. I thought the trade cycle might somehow be a stronger force than the prophecies of the then Prime Minister.

I therefore proposed that cathedrals with choir schools might take advantage of the then government's academy programme. Choir schools could be transferred to academy status. The cost of the school would be totally met by tax-payers. In return the cathedrals would offer centres of musical excellence to their dioceses and, in effect, to the surrounding state schools where music had largely died out.

A number of deans looked seriously at the proposal but were met with opposition from their choir school's governing body. Only one cathedral capitalized on this idea, which I had first written about in *The Sunday Times* on Christmas Eve 2006.

Bristol Cathedral choir school was facing significant financial challenges, due to Bristol having too many public schools for the size of the market the city could bear. The Chair of the Cathedral School, Stephen Parsons, phoned and asked when we could meet. I think he got on the train immediately and we planned how the Bristol Cathedral School could make an approach to Andrew Adonis, then Education Minister, to convert to academy status.

The school's story has been one of secure and wondrous advance ever since, although there are wreckers who wish to bring this success down by bogus applications to the Office of the Schools Adjudicator. These attempts have failed, although the legal costs have been high for the school. The school (now called Bristol Cathedral Choir School) is almost three times larger than it was before and now includes a cathedral primary school. In place of one boys' choir of twelve choristers and one part-time girls' choir, the cathedral now has two full-time choirs of eighteen boys and eighteen girls who sing the treble part with alto, tenor, and bass lay clerks.

The "Bristol" option is still open to cathedrals with choir schools and, as the screw is turned on cathedral accounts, maybe more will take that option and follow Bristol's way forward.

More recently I have suggested that the government's wish to establish free schools offers cathedrals again a line of advance which could be adopted both by cathedrals with choir schools and those without. It would be to establish, in a free school form, a series of cathedral schools.

The government has approved a cathedral multi-academy trust, which I chair, and wishes to see this development take place. The problem has been that cathedrals are anxious about embracing such an approach. At the time of writing we do not have a cathedral school up and running, so there is no cathedral school to which we can point to show how the idea can enhance a cathedral's role in its city and perhaps beyond.

This lack of faith is disappointing. I am just one of the people backing such a proposal: we have David Ross, the founder of Carphone Warehouse, and himself the driver of over thirty academies and free schools within his David Ross Education Trust. Tony Little, who was Headmaster of Eton, and now chairs a similar trust developing like David's, is also on our board of trustees. My work with the CFCE, I would have hoped, might have served as some hint of a track record of delivery.

But the proposal is delayed on the doubting-Thomas basis that unless the cathedral can put its collective finger, so to speak, into the side of a cathedral school, cathedrals collectively will not believe that such a development is possible. The Cathedral Academies Trust will persist in trying to give this proposal a good run for a number of reasons.

This free-school option is the last chance the Church will have significantly to increase its role in English education. The cathedral schools idea will add to the development of the cathedral's life and worship, as we wish these schools to be an integral part of the cathedral's life. Cathedrals have the chance of developing the ethos of cathedral schools which makes them distinct from others. Likewise, because of the involvement in the cathedral's life, pupils and parents and grandparents, and a wider family that may never have set foot inside a cathedral, will be turning up to all the main events of the cathedral school and therefore presenting, in the cathedral as well as within the school, a huge opportunity to mission for teaching about the faith.

———

Faith, of course, is a gift. But it seems that the Spirit finds it easier to impart this gift if we mere humans have done as much as we can to teach about the faith. In this task cathedrals play an important role, and that role could be expanded in the way that I have described in this foreword. But the other chapters of this volume also shout aloud how the cathedrals collectively have enhanced worship, income, hospitality, heritage, and —not to be laughed at—giving visitors a fun time. We neglect any link of faith and fun at our peril.

ACKNOWLEDGEMENTS

Bringing together such a varied selection of essays is both complex and time-consuming, and for that reason I would want to offer my warmest thanks to all the contributors who were faced with a fairly short deadline. Also, and primarily, I would like to thank Kay Norman, my Personal Assistant, who has worked endlessly and with great forbearance in bringing this collection to publication. My thanks also, as ever, to Rosslie, my wife, for all the support that she continues to give in all that I do, and for her work as the final copy editor, in preparation for sending the manuscript to our publisher.

Stephen Platten
Epiphany 2017

CONTENTS

CONTRIBUTORS

Stephen Platten is an Assistant Bishop in the Dioceses of London, Southwark, and Newcastle, and chairman of Hymns Ancient and Modern and of the governors of the Anglican Centre in Rome. He was formerly the Archbishop of Canterbury's Secretary for Ecumenical Affairs, Dean of Norwich, and Bishop of Wakefield. He was a member of the Cathedrals Fabric Commission for England from 2006 to 2016.

Peter Atkinson has been Dean of Worcester since 2007, having previously been a residentiary canon of Chichester, Principal of Chichester Theological College, and a parish priest in south London, Surrey, Bath, and Sussex. He is the author of two books, *Friendship and the Body of Christ* (2004) and *The Lion Encyclopaedia of the Bible* (2009).

Frank Field has been the Labour MP for Birkenhead since 1979. He chaired the Cathedrals Fabric Commission for England from 2005 to 2015 and founded the Cathedral Academies Trust in 2016.

Nicholas Henshall has been Dean of Chelmsford since 2014. He served as a parish priest for fourteen years in inner-city Newcastle, followed by six years as Canon Precentor of Derby Cathedral, and five as vicar of Christ Church, Harrogate. He worked for BBC local radio for six years and writes regularly for the Roman Catholic international weekly, *The Tablet*.

David Hoyle has been Dean of Bristol since 2010. Before that he had been a parish priest and more recently Canon Residentiary of Gloucester Cathedral and Secretary to the Theological Group of the House of Bishops.

He is a published historian and the author of *The Pattern of Our Calling* (2016).

Christopher Irvine is Canon Librarian and Director of Education at Canterbury Cathedral, and was formerly the Principal of the College of the Resurrection, Mirfield. He is a trustee of Art and Christianity Enquiry, and continues to teach Liturgical Studies. His previous publications include *The Use of Symbols in Worship* (2007) and *The Cross and Creation in Christian Liturgy and Art* (2013).

Jane Kennedy is architect to Ely, Newcastle, and Christ Church (Oxford) cathedrals and is also working with several Roman Catholic cathedrals. She is a senior partner at Purcell and is currently leading a team which is repairing, adapting, and extending Auckland Castle in County Durham to be a museum of faith.

Simon Oliver is Van Mildert Professor of Divinity at Durham University and Residentiary Canon of Durham Cathedral, having been on the faculty at Lampeter and then Associate Professor in the University of Nottingham. He specializes in systematic theology and philosophy. His most recent book is *Creation: A Guide for the Perplexed* (2017).

Jennie Page was for ten years (2006–2016) Vice Chair of the Cathedrals Fabric Commission for England, having been Chief Executive of English Heritage from 1989 to 1995. She is currently Vice Chair of the Church Buildings Council.

Richard Shephard was a member of Baroness Howe's Cathedrals Commission, whose report formed the basis of the 1999 Cathedrals Measure. Most recently he has been Director of the York Minster Trust and before that was Headmaster of the Minster School in York. He is a prolific composer of sacred music.

INTRODUCTION

How do different groups across the Church and wider society see cathedrals? Well, of course, the answer will be in multivarious ways, but here is just one answer to that question, included in *An Admonition to Parliament*, compiled in 1572 by Puritans under the leadership of Thomas Cartwright, sometime Professor of Divinity at the University of Cambridge. Cathedrals were, these Puritans perceived:

> the dennes of all loitering lubbers, where master Deane . . . Canons . . . the cheefe chaunter, singing men . . . squeaking queresters, organ players . . . live in great idleness, and have their abiding. If you would knowe whence all these came, we can easely answere you, that they came from the Pope, as oute of Trojan horse's bellye, to the destruction of God's kingdome. The churche of God never knewe them . . . [1]

Now, to say that the authors of this tract "had their own agenda" may be an understatement. Nonetheless, it is an indicator of how, in any age, cathedrals will be variously perceived. Even in the present day, it is clear that when statistics are quoted noting the growth and positive development of cathedrals, there are some in the "church growth lobby" who are irritated and dismissive. On the wider spectrum, they will argue that cathedrals are an irrelevance. Several of the essays that follow, however, indicate how—far from being an irrelevance—cathedrals are one area of the Church's life where increasingly the unchurched and the half-believer encounter God, and where the institutions of our society instinctively engage with the Christian gospel. They are *missionary* in any number of ways.

If one is to understand the vagaries of cathedral history over the centuries, Alan Mould's fascinating and detailed history of the chorister is a compact, entertaining, and perceptive guide to the perplexed. Whilst not being solely a history of music in cathedrals, its very subject matter lends itself to describing the varying fate of cathedrals down the centuries. It is fascinating to see how, with regard to cathedral life, the English Reformation(s)[2] was both conservative enough to preserve much of what went before and, with the re-founding of the monastic "cathedrals of the new foundation", to extend what was already extant in the secular cathedrals to those foundations which had formerly also been monastic houses. Certainly there were fallow periods for cathedral foundations. Mould cites, in more recent times, the eighteenth century as something of a nadir. Even then, however, he noted, for example:

> At Durham, perhaps uniquely, a weekly choral celebration
> of Holy Communion was maintained throughout the
> eighteenth century: a charming sketch of about 1780 shows
> such a celebration in progress with the surpliced choristers
> devoutly kneeling around the well-dressed altar.[3]

This complex and unpredictable history, alluded to with great bravura by David Hoyle in his essay in this volume, has contributed to the richness of the inheritance of English cathedral life. This is the third book in the past two decades which has reflected on cathedrals in England under a variety of headings. Pretentiously, this could be described as the final volume of a *trilogy* but that would assume a more strategic process than has been the case. Nonetheless, this book attempts to pick up new and largely different strands, as well as to complement the work set out in the two earlier volumes.[4] This brief introduction will not laboriously outline what follows chapter by chapter. Instead it will draw out three or four themes that these gathered essays uncover and which may be of use to all who value our cathedrals as they develop further in the coming decades.

Predictably, the issue of *finance* rears its head on more than one occasion, and in various essays. As this collection was being prepared, at least three cathedrals were struggling with financial difficulties; in at least one of our great cathedrals the financial issues were serious and strategic.

This raises issues of finance and governance; some have argued that the 1999 Cathedrals Measure did not deliver a financial/governance strategy that would offer advance warning signs before serious problems arose. A careful analysis of the Bishop of Peterborough's charge following his visitation, however, indicates that the 1999 Measure did indeed cover all the issues he raises;[5] the cathedral had failed to adhere to the substance and requirements of the measure. Such failures need to be faced in the near future in a manner which appropriately respects the independence of cathedral foundations, allows the chapter to remain the proper governing body (under the leadership of the dean), and at the same time produces a strategy with sufficient teeth to intervene when the financial policy appears to be flawed.[6] A proper independence of cathedral foundations is an asset and not a weakness within diocesan and capitular structures and governance.

The availability of grants for fabric from English Heritage, and more recently from the Heritage Lottery Fund, together with the First World War grants from H. M. Treasury have been of great benefit. The increasing demands of tourism, however, have pressed for facilities that cannot be funded by grants offered by the state. If one adds to this the increasing difficulties that some foundations have in advancing the growth of capitular revenues annually, then critical times are ahead. Earlier in the twentieth century, Frank Bennett, the great reforming Dean of Chester, led the way in opening cathedrals up to a wider public and removing entrance charges.[7] Contemporary pressures have begun to reverse this process in a number of places. This development, understandable as it is, with financial issues ever looming, has theological as well as practical implications. Cathedrals are often seen as "gracious courts" where all may roam freely, transcendent common ground—holy ground even. To allow all to enter our cathedrals, or at least part of each cathedral, is a sign of God's grace, God's free gift to all humanity, as exemplified supremely and uniquely in the incarnation of Jesus Christ: God empties of all to come among us as one of us. With the financial challenges facing them, how will our cathedrals seek still to offer all or part of their buildings freely to all who come?

Ironically, a second key theme is almost the polar opposite. Very often, cathedrals are seen as the "fat cats" of the Church of England and maybe of the Church of God more widely. They are better resourced in terms of staff, in their musical foundation, often in estate (where there is a close or precinct), in the great building itself, and in reputation, as the focal point, the flagship of the Spirit for their region, than the average parish church. This places a dual challenge or responsibility on those who govern and administer cathedrals. How can the diocese be better embraced and welcomed? How can the cathedral foundation benefit the diocese more widely, including the parishes? Interestingly enough, this is a two-way process. It is not only cathedrals who are myopic. Many years ago, while Dean of Norwich, I tried to get round to all deanery chapters in the diocese over a period of time. I visited one deanery, only eight or nine miles to the west of the city. At the end of a two-hour session, much of which was question and answer, one priest reflected: "Well, thank you for coming—of course, the cathedral has little real relevance to us this far out of the city!" It is not, however, only within the Church that perceptions need to be challenged. The wider community also can too easily see cathedrals as the preserve of the rich. A willingness to engage with issues of social ethics and community support is one way of offering a more prophetic face to the world.

Both these issues about perception within and outside the church community also relate to how cathedrals see themselves. A significant number of our cathedrals are former parish churches and indeed still have responsibility for a parish, that is, a designated geographical area of responsibility and reference. But even with this group of cathedrals, the parish is not the paramount role. Too much of a focus on the parish and its administration, or on the cathedral congregation in non-parochial cathedrals, will distract the foundation from its focus in the wider city, area, and region. It may also engender an inward-looking tendency which can lean towards overmuch interiorized reflection on the "home community". Cathedral congregations are part of the life-blood of the great foundations, but they are not its sole raison d'être. Cathedrals have no need to imitate the work of parish churches: there is plenty of choice there for all. Instead, the congregations themselves need to be outward-looking, offering a real missionary ministry to the wider community.

Finally, there is much positivity, in the light of the foregoing, which allows cathedrals to celebrate their freedom to do new things. They can be neutral ground, where people may come together to explore and debate the key social and political issues of our age. This will not avoid controversy and can often lead to some stress and the expending of much nervous energy. One cathedral hosted a conference on the ethics of genetically modified foods: the chapter email system was effectively jammed for a week or more by those opposed to GM food. Cathedrals can be centres of excellence in so many areas—music, liturgy, architectural development, Christian education—and often in a specific area where there has been a particular focus: Coventry's focus on reconciliation is one vivid example, but there are many more. Again, such excellence is to be shared and made available to all, both within and outside the church community. Cathedrals can offer vision and leadership within the wider region—what sort of Borchester would you like to leave as a legacy to your grandchildren? How can the insights and imperatives of the Christian gospel nourish such a vision in a manner that is generous to all, of any faith or none. It was prophetic that Sadiq Khan, the Muslim Mayor of London, should inaugurate his new work at Southwark Cathedral. That spoke of a generosity of Mayor and Cathedral alike.

The broad themes identified here are by no means exhaustive, but they do arise in different ways in the essays that follow. They do hint that in allowing our cathedrals to be imaginatively open to the widest of worlds, we are inviting those who come to tread with confidence and with a positive fear and trembling, for they will be treading on holy ground.

Stephen Platten
Cornhill, London, Epiphany 2017

NOTES

1. Quoted in Alan Mould, *The English Chorister: A History* (Bloomsbury Continuum, 2007). Cited earlier in W. H. Frere and C .E. Douglas (ed. Norman Sykes), *Puritan Manifestos* (Church History Society, 1954), clause 17, p. 32.
2. Christopher Haigh, in his interesting monograph, *English Reformations* (Oxford University Press, 1993), argues that there was no "single" Reformation

in England; similar themes emerge in the work of Diarmaid MacCulloch: *Thomas Cranmer: A Life* (Yale University Press, 1998) and *Tudor Church Militant* (Penguin, 1999). The Henrician, Edwardian, Marian, and Elizabethan periods all contributed to a longer and more complex process of Reformation in England. See also Chapter 4 in this volume and especially notes 35 and 36.

3. Mould, *The English Chorister*, p. 146.

4. Stephen Platten and Christopher Lewis (eds.), *Flagships of the Spirit: Cathedrals in Society* (Darton, Longman and Todd, 1998), and Stephen Platten and Christopher Lewis (eds.), *Dreaming Spires? Cathedrals in a New Age* (SPCK, 2006).

5. Cf. "The Bishop's Visitation Charge to Peterborough Cathedral", January 2017 (<https://www.peterborough-cathedral.org.uk>).

6. See Angela Tilby's excellent article, "Bishops, Leave These Deans Alone", *Church Times*, 3 February 2017, p. 13.

7. Here cf. Alex Bruce, *The Cathedral "Open and Free": Dean Bennett of Chester* (Liverpool Historical Studies, Liverpool University Press, 2000).

1. CATHEDRALS—WHAT'S THE POINT?

Stephen Platten

Alongside asking clergy to "Say one for me", or reflecting that Sunday's coming up and it's "your busy day", people are now commenting cheerily that, when they go for their weekly supermarket shop and come to the cheese counter, they always opt for Cathedral City Cheddar. It is the most popular cheese by sales, statistics tell us. There is an amusing irony here, inasmuch as all Cathedral City Cheddar is made at a creamery in the village of Davidstow in Cornwall, nowhere near a cathedral. Indeed, even if it were made in Cheddar, it would not be next door to a cathedral city, although Wells would not be far away. Upon which cathedral city is the manufacturer focusing?

Ask aficionados of cathedrals which is their favourite and most often they are stumped—between the glories of so many, they cannot make a sharp choice—unless, that is, they were born in a cathedral city to which, of course, they cannot but have loyalty. Look for the best-situated cathedral in England, and then arguably the prize must go to Lincoln. Arrayed like a great ocean liner on the cliff which passes north to south through Lincolnshire, it can be seen for fifteen or twenty miles, even from the Great North Road, on a clear day. Of a winter's evening it glows as it is floodlit on its hill. Interestingly enough, it's Lincoln that is featured on Cathedral City Cheddar adverts! But other cathedrals come into their own from the railway—Truro's three spires, Durham's three towers standing on the bluff above the river. Wakefield can boast the tallest spire in Yorkshire and Bury St Edmunds' magnificent twentieth-century Gothic tower proclaims that this is the cathedral of Suffolk. Derby's powerful

Perpendicular tower with James Gibb's Neo-Classical church contrasts with most people's expectations of a midland industrial centre. So what precisely is a "cathedral city" and why does the word "cathedral" mark off such places with a distinct aura?

CATHEDRALS AND PLACE

In September 2014, English Heritage (for these purposes now Historic England) published a report, the origins of which had been an enquiry into the life and sustainability of English cathedral cities.[1] The initiative to produce the report owed much to the energy of both the Earl of March and Dr Simon Thurley, then Director of English Heritage; it was accompanied by a series of seminars. These seminars gathered together distinguished architects alongside representatives of other interested agencies and parties, including representatives of the Cathedrals Fabric Commission for England. These discussions were both fascinating and revealing, and uncovered several areas where mainland continental countries have been more effective than Britain in encouraging sustainable development in such communities. Perhaps most interesting for this volume of essays was their starting point. Cathedral cities (and that includes some "cathedral towns") are seen to have a particular cachet within our national culture. The report did not focus narrowly on cathedrals themselves, but rather on the organic development of these communities rooted particularly in the built environment. This was not purely an historical and architectural study. It focused on the life of these towns historically and in the present day. It concerned itself with place.

In 2015, the results of a rather different European study were published as a collection of essays issuing from the so-called "Heimat Study", which brought together experts from a variety of fields including ecology, planning, landscape design, philosophy, theology, public policy, and anthropology.[2] Once again, at the heart of the study was a focus on *place*. Place is understood dynamically and includes a proper appreciation of the cultural history, ecology, and demography that has given life and shape to a particular human community. In the introductory chapter, particularly focusing on the Dearne Valley in South Yorkshire, the two editors opine thus: "... there were some very partial and impoverished understandings of "community" ... and how this related to the meanings of place—and how communities related to meanings of place."[3] Later in the book, Professor John Rodwell adverts further to these issues, and particularly in relation to the cherishing—or indeed ignoring—of social and industrial history within the Dearne Valley. The argument which stands at the heart of the book, however, goes well beyond one post-industrial region of Yorkshire. The study included writers from Norway, Germany, and Sweden. Similar critiques are offered of other localities.

Both these recent studies can well inform all who would reflect upon the nature and life of cathedrals and their environments, for in so many cases, the character of these towns and cities is encapsulated in their cathedral churches: the celebrated photograph of St Paul's Cathedral, in the 1940s during the Blitz, and of Coventry after the Baedeker raid; the photograph of Ely Cathedral rising out of the mist as the "Ship of the Fens", and the logo of the former Norwich Union Insurance Company immortalizing the cathedral there; the tower of Portsmouth Cathedral standing as a safe haven for sailors, or the crown spire of Newcastle Cathedral acting as an emblem for that estimable capital of England's North East. Similar reflections could be made about every other English cathedral to a greater or lesser extent. Cathedrals, time after time, are icons or symbols of the places in which they are situated.

CATHEDRALS AS ORGANIC

Of course, following from that, they can all too easily be identified as splendid heritage buildings to be placed alongside castles and stately homes, or the noble civic galleries and city halls of northern England. Seen as such, especially with the growth of the conservation lobby, it is but one step into a precious and static understanding of what are indeed organic buildings bringing with them an extraordinarily dynamic past, a past which includes warts and inconsistencies, alongside jewels, diadems, and perfect symmetry. One example will suffice. In the mid-1990s, it was decided to plan new developments within the historic footprint of Norwich Cathedral. This would ultimately be the largest single development within a mediaeval English cathedral since the Reformation. But that impressive statement conceals ten years of spirited debate. One tiny element captures the process. In the 1960s, the south nave Romanesque blind arcading had been pierced to allow access from the nave into the adjoining locutory, which would then become the shop. This access point was a key factor in the new development. It would allow access from the re-animated cloister buildings to and from the cathedral church without changes in level. Despite equivalence in levels, its width precluded the passage of wheelchairs, the very reason for wishing to use it. The development architect proposed an ingenious and simple remedy: produce a wider modified Romanesque soffit. Purists deplored such heresy; it would be a complete anomaly and a nonsense. Before bowing to such an opinion, however, turn and look north-west into the nave. There, for all to see, is a Gothic arch ill-fitted into an earlier Romanesque doorway. Just a little higher up one can see the two string courses running along the north and south tribune galleries. They are out of kilter and manifestly so—the northern triforium is perceptibly some inches higher than the south. Some seven years on, after consulting with all the statutory agencies and discarding all other possibilities, the architect's solution was agreed and completed.

It is something of a parable: cathedrals are undoubtedly symbolic of the places in which they are set and of their history, but they are organic living buildings too. Developments and lessons learnt need not be expunged. Instead they can be models of how we cherish our wider cultural history, even those facets of it which we in later generations feel could have been better, less ugly, closer to perfection. The manicured lawns preferred by the now defunct Ministry of Public Buildings and Works have more recently, in places, given way to wild gardens and areas of meadow—so too with National Trust properties. Cathedrals may still have lessons to learn both within their buildings and outside within their landscapes or townscapes. But this model of organic growth goes deeper still, for cathedrals are not merely symbolic of their cities. They are also de facto *holy places.* It is only fairly recently that real attention has been focused here. The last decade of the twentieth century and the early part of this century have seen proper studies of churches and cathedrals as both iconic of their wider communities but also as breathing an historically and spiritually organic life.[4] That life, too, will have its warts, blemishes, and inconsistencies: history is never a perfectly moral staircase into the present. Acknowledging human fallibility alongside celebrating humanity's holiest aspirations is something for which cathedrals have a unique potential and capacity.

Cathedrals, then, in common with all church buildings, as noted in the recent review by the Church of England's Church Buildings Review Group, are shaped essentially by their setting and by place, and the people associated with that place both historically and within the present day. The Church is often seen only as "the people", but the buildings within which they worship are a key part of the wider environment and point, almost sacramentally,[5] to the God of our Lord Jesus Christ for whose worship they were built.

PLACE, WORSHIP, AND THE OPUS DEI

The primary purpose, then, of both parish church and cathedral is to be a place of worship, a place where people gather to celebrate the church's liturgy through words, music, silence, symbols, and sacramental signs. As places of worship, church buildings are places where the triune God is invoked and expressed. It is what *happens* on these occasions that makes the building a holy place.[6] There is, however, more to add, remembering the distinctive roles played by cathedrals both within the Church and also in relation to wider society. That sense of place has a contemporary resonance as cathedrals perform the role of "flagships of the spirit" within a local community.[7]

Most church buildings are palimpsests, where successive historical periods have added the story of their own particular local communities. Many such buildings, including a number of cathedrals, receive their individuality through the stories of particular saints or holy people. Indeed, it is association with such stories which adds to their sense of being holy places. So, the essential importance of *place* in understanding the significance of church buildings has been established. However, place in itself has also been seen only as a necessary and not a sufficient condition for exploring the raison d'être of church buildings, including cathedrals.

Perhaps the most vivid example is the basilica of St Peter in Rome. In visiting St Peter's, it is possible to tour the buildings which predate the present sixteenth-century monumental basilica and, within the so-called *Scavi*,[8] to walk down a first-century street. The key to this visit is, of course, to discover the original tomb of St Peter, following his martyrdom.[9] Ironically in at least one other case, however, the holiness of the building and its crucial attraction as a centre of pilgrimage is based entirely on an event for which there is no evidence. This case is, of course, the story of the bringing of the body of St James the Great from the Holy Land to Santiago de Compostela in north-west Spain. The body was not even putatively discovered until the ninth century, and a legend of its early translation in the first century grew up around this. The thinness of the evidence for the translation of St James' remains, however, has not stopped this place from becoming one of the prime pilgrim sites in Christendom. Indeed, it is pilgrimage itself that has endowed the cathedral with its now undisputed holiness as a focus for pilgrimage.[10]

SAINTS, PILGRIMAGE, AND PLACE

In England there are similar examples of buildings gaining their pre-eminence through the story of an individual saint. One of the earliest examples is Durham where, after a journey—perhaps longer than any he made during his lifetime—St Cuthbert's body was laid to rest in Durham Cathedral, where it remains. In early mediaeval times Durham Cathedral became a great centre of pilgrimage. Or again elsewhere, and later in mediaeval times, following his violent death in 1170 Thomas Becket was canonized and his shrine became a great centre of pilgrimage. The

Pilgrim's Way across southern England gave to Canterbury Cathedral a still greater significance than it already had as the seat of St Augustine. Similar if less dramatic stories relate to St Richard at Chichester, St Frideswide in Oxford, St Swithun in Winchester, St Chad in Lichfield, St Hugh in Lincoln, St Osmond in Salisbury, and St Alban in his eponymous abbey and cathedral. Elsewhere, less well-known saints led to the erection of shrines which would remodel the buildings themselves. Less happy stories relate to "Little St Hugh" of Lincoln and the attempts to canonize the child murder victim, William, at Norwich. In these cases an anti-semitic tale was concocted in an attempt to produce a martyr saint to further the significance of the cathedral. The crucial interpretation of pilgrimage and the sophisticated related theology remains, then, an essential element in understanding the nature of cathedrals.

Remarkably, recent times have seen a dramatic resurgence of interest in pilgrimage, and as indicated above, cathedrals have become the major foci and destinations for pilgrims. A recent account of the revival of pilgrimage has suggested that the phenomenon of pilgrimage, as distinct from spiritual tourism, has three basic elements.

First, coming to a place of pilgrimage may well situate the visitor or pilgrim in a place where prayer is not only possible but enriched by the associations with the saint. At a pilgrim site visitors can find themselves in a place where, as T. S. Eliot reflected, in an oft-repeated phrase, "prayer has been valid." In the very act of placing themselves there, they may discover that prayer is intensified, made more real, made more immediate as they find themselves on "holy ground". Second, journeying to a pilgrim shrine may help us to recover the sheer physicality of Christian life, and the importance of touch in the life and practice of prayer for the embodied Christian. Third, coming to a traditional pilgrimage site may well reawaken in the pilgrim a sense of how our individual lives are bound up and knitted together with a "cloud of witnesses", and that one participates in a wider society, the communion of saints that straddles heaven and earth.[11]

There is one further key concept with which to engage in understanding cathedrals and pilgrimage, and that is the concept of liminality. This relates to the above three elements but presses beyond them. Pilgrimage is a liminal concept inasmuch as it relates to approaching a threshold which one then crosses. In crossing the threshold there is a transformation.

One's perception and experience are changed and there is an element of challenge within this. It is easy to underestimate how strange and even frightening it can be for those unused to churches and churchgoing simply to cross that threshold. More positively, however, that challenge can be spiritually transformational. The experience of journeying on the *camino* to Santiago de Compostela in Spain, and completing that journey, has been at the heart of pilgrimage over the centuries. Even the symbol of the scallop shell captures something of this. Mediaeval pilgrims marked their fulfilment of the pilgrimage to Compostela by journeying a further twenty miles or so to the beach, where legend has it the body of St James was landed. Here they would gather to themselves a scallop shell as a mark of having crossed that key threshold at the shrine of the saint.

As we have seen, it would be naïve, however, to suggest that pilgrimage in relation to cathedrals concludes at the great west door. Canterbury, for example, by its very internal design, causes the visitor to become a pilgrim moving through the womb-like nave, up the steps past the place of the martyrdom of Thomas Becket, notably at the *crossing*, and then finally up into the choir and Trinity Chapel, the place of the Holy Spirit and the saints. In that pilgrimage within the building, Canterbury Cathedral is itself a potent model of the Holy Trinity. Further, it should be said that the intentional pilgrim brings to the site of pilgrimage the places and communities to which he or she belongs, and from which they have come, and thereby adds to the sediment of a "holy place".

Similar reflections can be made about other cathedrals and the journey the visitor or pilgrim makes to the shrine. This presses home a crucial element in understanding the theology of cathedral buildings, inasmuch as there is in every case the possibility of a narrative by means of which visitors are encouraged to circulate through the building. In Durham, for example, one may be a pilgrim in one of two directions, either beginning in the west at the tomb of Bede, and proceeding through the building to the shrine of St Cuthbert, or taking the opposite journey beginning at Cuthbert's shrine. Both directions are telling, and in each case the building will speak theologically of the Christian faith.

One should add that the association of cathedrals with individuals will not always focus strictly upon pilgrimage, but rather on the historical significance of both religious and secular figures. So Bishop Edward King's statue in Lincoln reminds visitors of the powerful pastoral inheritance of Bishop King; Launcelot Andrewes' tomb in Southwark Cathedral has been a focus of prayer, remembering Andrewes' own devotional witness; Chichester's Arundel Screen reminds visitors of George Bell's prophetic witness to peace and unity amongst the nations. Secular figures are significant too. The tombs of Katherine of Aragon, Prince Arthur and King John, and King Edward II in Peterborough, Worcester, and Gloucester cathedrals respectively are but four examples; more recently, of course, there has been the celebrated discovery of the remains of King Richard III and their reburial in Leicester Cathedral—some considerable energy was expended to make it clear that Richard's tomb was not to be seen as a focus of pilgrimage.

Indeed, the interrelationship between building and theology and also between building and liturgy raises key issues. The way in which a building is used for worship is, to a degree, fashioned by the internal design and ground-plan of the building. Equally, the essential requirements of liturgy (and in a cathedral liturgies will be many and various) will pattern the manner in which the building is both prayed in and used for worship. Salisbury, for instance, is well known for its processional and stational liturgies, such as the Advent Procession and diocesan services of Christian initiation.[12] The situation of the cathedral within its wider environment becomes part of the inductive approach in relation to how theology relates to each cathedral building. These issues will be explained in more detail further on in this book.

This interrelationship prompts discussion of a phrase frequently used of cathedrals: they are described as both *sacred space* and *common ground*.[13] Already we have alluded to the use of sacred space; there has recently come about a renewed awareness of the importance of this term. At times there has been a tension between sacred space and common ground. In the twentieth century there was a reluctance to allow the "secular" to invade religious buildings. It is clear, however, that throughout history there has been an oscillation in church buildings (and notably in cathedrals) between the sacred and the secular. Often the nave of a cathedral was the "people's church". Certainly this was manifestly the case in monastic cathedrals where the monks' domain often lay beyond the pulpitum or screen.

PUBLIC THEOLOGY AND PUBLIC PRAYER

This reminds us of the key role played in the development of one of the two traditions of the divine office as it developed through time. The "cathedral office" was celebrated daily by the cathedral community either of secular canons, or of a monastic chapter. As George Guiver CR has argued, these celebrations of daily prayer are probably best described as a "people's office" because of their participatory character.[14]

Books were unknown in this tradition, and it has been argued that the development of books for use in the divine office contributed to the "privatization" of the office in mediaeval times.[15] Certainly this tradition of prayer lends another essential strand to a theological/liturgical understanding of cathedrals. They are classically buildings focused on public prayer.[16] Cranmer's revision and conflation of the monastic office into Morning and Evening Prayer was intended to engage laity in daily worship. One of the unintended outcomes of this tradition within a musical context has been the remarkable flowering of Choral Evensong, which remains a unique feature of English cathedrals and which has acted as a school for professional musicians. Many singers, instrumentalists, and orchestral conductors have begun their musical careers as cathedral choristers.

But the *common ground* element within the equation also contributes its own theological strand, and not only with the impact of visitors, tourists, and pilgrims, but also on what is now described as "public theology". Cathedrals are natural centres for debate on key social issues: the international debt crisis, GM farming, urban theology etc. This is just one way in which cathedrals may exist as common ground, that is, somewhere where all may come—without political attachment—and openly discuss the relationship of society to such issues. Cathedrals are also places of creativity and artistic skill, where people continue to work in stone, wood, stained glass, and painting. Cathedrals not only continue to commission new works of art, but also increasingly host art exhibitions of imaginative depth to challenge and inspire significant numbers of visitors. In these ways, the building allows a natural impact of theology on the public debates of social and cultural value.[17]

More locally, a cathedral may allow society in that place to reflect upon itself. In Norfolk, issues of redesigning the coastline have been debated. In Truro, the distinctive nature of Cornish history and culture has been a key issue within the cathedral's life and a determinant of the nature of its ministry.[18] In Blackburn, William Temple's key concern for a cathedral and diocese which both reflected accurately and also allowed the development of Lancashire's own character played a crucial part in the fashioning of the new cathedral there.[19] In Coventry Cathedral, an account of the dramatic destruction of the mediaeval building there has produced an enduring focus on peace and reconciliation. The Community of the Cross of Nails, the links with Dresden and the *Frauenkirche*, and the appointment of a Residentiary Canon focusing upon this work are powerful indicators: the ruins of the earlier cathedral are themselves iconic.[20] Manchester, from the time of Dean Jowett onwards, has been committed to effective pan-European links. York Minster retains a focal ecumenical link with the historic relationship between the first Earl of Halifax and the Abbé Portal and Cardinal Mercier of Malines in Belgium.

In almost every cathedral, theology is further affected by the panoply of stakeholders who believe the cathedral to be *their* cathedral. From the local Rotary Club to the County or Unitary Council, from voluntary agencies to civic events, from the local university to countless schools—the number of stakeholders is myriad and each stakeholder will add something to the "public theological" impact of the cathedral.

In being the focus for many stakeholders, cathedrals are also "buildings for all seasons". At Advent and Christmas, many local agencies and businesses choose the cathedral for their carol service. In more rural dioceses, Rogationtide and Harvest will be focuses. In Holy Week, the cathedral will often be the place of worship for people of all Christian traditions. Finally, in national and international crises, cathedrals will be foci, acting as ventricles within the "nation's heart" as it responds to tragedy or celebration. The response to the death of Diana, Princess of Wales is one obvious example. Books of condolence, candle-stands, and buildings "open all hours" characterized another key role, this time in relating the local to the national and international.

THEOLOGICAL ORIGINS

Rather late in the day, perhaps, in these initial reflections on the nature of cathedrals, we need a potent reminder that the *essential* definition of a cathedral is that it is the "seat of the bishop".[21] The bishop is both the local "focus of unity" for the Church and even, to some extent, for the wider community. But by dint of the bishop being part of the national and international college of bishops, cathedrals speak of the universal Church and, to use that popular cliché, the global village.[22] Archbishop Robert Runcie, in his international visits throughout the Anglican Communion, frequently preached about "the Lord, the locals, and the link". The bishop, he noted, was both the local focus of unity but also the living representative of that place in the universal Church. Very often the sermon would be delivered in the cathedral, the enduring sign of local unity and international collegiality. This in itself needs to be viewed as a key part of ecclesiological reflection. Cathedrals are indeed "ecclesiological buildings"! This is a key issue to remember when diocesan boundaries are reconsidered in the light of changes in demography over time. It may make better ecclesiological sense to federate dioceses rather than consolidate them in such a manner as to proliferate cathedrals as multiple foci within one diocese.

As well as focusing the local and universal, cathedrals also, through their ministry to visitors and tourists, touch upon implicit religion. This may be one of the ways of distinguishing the different but related roles of bishop and dean. The role of the bishop has been rehearsed briefly in relation to ecclesiology. The decanal role, within the broader chapter, is to focus key issues of a secular nature within the locality, within and alongside the dean's liturgical roles. With the local chapter, the dean may then sense those issues which are resonant locally and also identify implicit religious pulses within which the cathedral may work as part of its missionary strategy. Through the regular pattern of public prayer, cathedrals point to the essence of Christian "spirituality". As this essential public prayer infuses the implicit religion, cathedrals are paramount reminders of the importance, in western secularized societies, of "vicarious religion", to use a term frequently employed by the sociologists of religion.[23] They are the most obvious examples of the expression of "believing without belonging".

This point may well indicate why cathedrals have, over the past twenty years, been one of the key growth points in the Church of England. They are places where people may worship without the sort of commitment often assumed to be required in parish churches. Anonymity can often be preserved along with the avoidance of the frustrating petty politics of many small communities. This growth continues and stands in stark contrast to the picture of cathedrals gleaned from histories of the Victorian Church.[24]

In the variety of ways outlined above, cathedral communities have begun to reflect on their theological and liturgical raison d'être. Cathedrals are now far more aware than in the past of the context of their own city and how that shapes the mission and ministry in their particular place; this in turn speaks to a theological understanding of the building. Liturgy and worship have been approached with much clearer theological analysis than was true even half a century ago. The advent of the worldwide Liturgical Movement in the mid-twentieth century and, more specifically within the Church of England, the work of the Liturgical Commission have led to a proper theological analysis of the theory and practice of worship. Cathedrals have become nurseries and even laboratories of liturgical theology and practice. The rebirth of pilgrimage as a theme across all the churches has directed cathedrals to a proper "theology of place". This, combined with an appreciation of the sense of sacred space and common ground in their unique containment of vast transcendental space, has led to a further theological/sociological analysis of the role of a cathedral. In turn, the significance of regular public worship has been reinforced; the saying/singing of the daily office is both a mark of continuity and also speaks to the contemporary world.

Alongside this, the increased focus on "episcopal services" (perhaps most notably in the flowering of cathedral baptisms and confirmations) has reinforced the theology of episcopacy. Bishops are the focus of unity for the local church, that is, the diocese; a cathedral is by definition the seat of the bishop: here is the *cathedra*. Increasingly, the cathedral has become a centre for the bishop as teacher: many bishops now lead Lenten studies and also use the cathedral as a focus for other educational work. Some cathedrals have, by circumstance, become a focus of a particular strand of theology.

Finally, a potent manifestation of this greater sense of theological purpose has been in the completion of a series of "big books", outlining the history, development, and current role of individual cathedrals— Canterbury, York, Norwich, Worcester, Hereford, Ely, and Coventry are just some examples.[25] These studies continue. The publication of monographs on the role of cathedrals,[26] of which this is but one, is a further example of theological reflection. It will be important for such reflections to remain open and not over-deductive or prescriptive. Here the Church of England, with its in-built tendency towards an inductive approach to theology, can speak with a growing theological intelligence by reflecting upon its cathedrals and their ministry.

NOTES

1. The report was finally published in October 2014 by English Heritage (this section of the former body is now known as Historic England) under the title, *The Sustainable Growth of Cathedral Cities and Historic Towns* (available to download from <https://www.historicengland.org.uk/images-books/publications/sustainable-growth-of-cathedral-cities-and-historic-towns>).

2. John Rodwell and Peter Manley Scott (eds.), *At Home in the Future: Place and Belonging in a Changing Europe*, (Lit Verlag, 2015). N.B. The German word *Heimat* includes a rich variety of resonances relating to "home ground" and the importance of history, landscape, and context of *place* in the human community.

3. Rodwell and Scott, *At Home in the Future*, p. 1.

4. Cf. John Inge, *A Christian Theology of Place* (Ashgate, 2003); Philip Sheldrake, *Spaces for the Sacred: Place, Memory and Identity* (SCM Press, 2001); Timothy Gorringe, *A Theology of the Built Environment: Justice, Empowerment, Redemption* (Cambridge University Press, 2002). Cf. also *Report of the Church Buildings Review Group* (The Church of England, 2015, available online at <https://www.churchofengland.org/media/2383717/church_buildings_review_report_2015.pdf>), and especially the theological analysis by the Bishop of Worcester, the Rt Revd John Inge.

5. Cf. Stephen Platten, "Building Sacraments", in *Theology*, Vol. 117 No. 2 (2014), pp. 83–93.

6. It is what happens within the walls of the building, the prayer and worship, that makes the *domus ecclesiae*, house of the people of God, a *domus Dei*, a house of God. Cf. Christopher Irvine, "Space", Chapter 11 in Juliette Day and Benjamin Gordon-Taylor (eds.), *The Study of Liturgy and Worship* (SPCK, 2013).

7. Cf. Stephen Platten and Christopher Lewis (eds.), *Flagships of the Spirit: Cathedrals in Society* (Darton, Longman and Todd, 1998).

8. The *Scavi* are the excavated remains of a first-century cemetery centred on one particular street, the Via Cornelia. It is believed that St Peter was buried here, having been martyred in the nearby Circus of Nero. In the twentieth century extensive excavations were carried out, from 1940 to 1949 during the pontificate of Pope Pius XII. Further excavations, in 2003, have revealed more. See, for example, P. Liverani, G. Spinola, and P. Zander, *The Vatican Necropoles: Rome's City of the Dead* (Brepols, 2010).

9. Cf. Martin Warner (ed.), *Say Yes to God: Mary and the Revealing of the Word Made Flesh* (Tufton Books, 1999), especially Section 5, "Revealed in the Liturgy", and Stephen Platten, "Cathedrals: Sacred Spaces and Common Ground", pp. 181ff.

10. Ibid., p. 183.

11. Christopher Irvine, "Canterbury Cathedral: Pilgrims and cathedrals as places of pilgrimage" in *Theology* Vol. 118 No. 6 (2015), pp. 421–428.

12. Platten, "Building Sacraments", pp. 83–93.

13. Wesley Carr (ed.), *Say One for Me: The Church of England in the Next Decade* (SPCK, 1992).

14. George Guiver CR, *Company of Voices: Daily Prayer and the People of God* (SPCK, 1998, revised edn. Canterbury Press, 2001), Chapters 8–12.

15. Robert Taft and Joseph Jungmann, *Christian Prayer through the Centuries* (SPCK, 2007).

16. Platten and Lewis, *Flagships of the Spirit*, pp. 130ff.

17. Cf. Fraser Watts, "Coventry Cathedral: A Theology of Society", in *Theology*, Vol. 118 No. 6 (2015), pp. 429–437.

18. Linda Barley, "Truro Cathedral: Spires of Hope in the Duchy Peninsula", in *Theology*, Vol. 118 No. 6 (2015), pp. 404–412.

19. Ian Stockton, "Blackburn Cathedral: William Temple's vision for a new see and cathedral finally fulfilled", in *Theology*, Vol. 118 No. 6 (2015), pp. 413–420.

20. Fraser Watts, "Coventry Cathedral".

21. Platten and Lewis, *Flagships of the Spirit*, pp. 128ff.

22. See also here the key issues raised by "communion" theologies rooted in ecumenical dialogue. Cf. Stephen Platten and Christopher Lewis (eds.), *Dreaming Spires: Cathedrals in a New Age* (SPCK, 2006), especially pp. 6ff.

23. Cf. Grace Davie, *Europe: The Exceptional Case* (Darton, Longman and Todd, 2002) especially Chapters 1 and 6.

24. Cf. Owen Chadwick, *The Victorian Church*, especially Vol. 2 (Black, 1970), pp. 366–395, and Edward Meyrick Goulburn, ed. Noel Henderson, *The Goulburn Norwich Diaries* (Canterbury Press, 1996), passim.

25. Patrick Collinson, Nigel Ramsay, and Margaret Sparks (eds.), *A History of Canterbury Cathedral* (OUP, 1995); G. E. Aylmer and Reginald Cant (eds.), *A History of York Minster* (Clarendon Press, 1977); Ian Atherton, Eric Fernie, Christopher Harper-Bill, and Hassell Smith (eds.), *Norwich Cathedral: Church, City and Diocese, 1096–1996* (The Hambledon Press, 1996); Ute Engel, *Worcester Cathedral: An Architectural History* (Phillimore and Co. Ltd, 2007); Christopher Lamb, *Reconciling People: Coventry Cathedral's Story* (Canterbury Press, 2011). In Ireland, too, there is at least one example, in Kenneth Milne, *Christ Church Cathedral Dublin: A History* (Four Courts Press Ltd, 2000).

26. Iain M. MacKenzie (ed.), *Cathedrals Now: Their Use and Place in Society* (Canterbury Press, 1996); Platten and Lewis (eds.), *Flagships of the Spirit*; Platten and Lewis (eds.) *Dreaming Spires*.

2. THE CATHEDRAL AND ROOTED GROWTH

Simon Oliver

CATHEDRALS AND GROWTH

Numerous statistical and qualitative reports in recent years indicate modest but persistent growth in cathedral congregations since the millennium. At the time of writing, the most recent set of cathedral statistics shows an average weekly attendance at services in 2015 to be 36,700 adults and children. This is an increase of 18 per cent from 31,200 in 2005. Easter communicants in 2015 were at their highest level since 2009. Attendance at cathedral services during Advent in 2015 (the period from Advent Sunday to 23 December) stood at 824,000, the highest level for a decade. There were 9.4 million visits to cathedrals in 2015. The number of people volunteering at cathedrals has risen by 13 per cent from 13,300 in 2005 to 15,000 in 2015.[1] Many reasons have been given to explain the durability of cathedral congregations, including the quality of the music, the grandeur of the setting, and the variety of worship and events on offer within a relatively well-resourced Christian community. Recent statistics indicate that attendance at mid-week services keeps cathedral congregations buoyant. Intuitively, this makes sense: cathedrals are often situated in the centre of cities, which makes access during the working day very easy for a large number of people. An increasing range of non-church Sunday activities for families means that worship during the week becomes

an attractive option. Cathedrals also have a number of other daytime
attractions—lectures, recitals, exhibitions, a shop and restaurant—which
encourage a mid-week following.

A robust qualitative study of cathedral life published in 2012 by the
think-tank Theos and The Grubb Institute, entitled "Spiritual Capital: The
Present and Future of English Cathedrals", also points to the vibrant and
growing life of cathedrals.[2] The report indicates that 27 per cent of the
resident adult population in England visited a cathedral during the year of
the survey (September 2011 to October 2012). Of the many conclusions
and recommendations of the report, I should like to highlight two. First,
cathedrals play a vital role within their regional communities as a source
of "bridging" social capital.[3] They establish and encourage relationships
between a variety of community groups, including charities, schools,
unions, local government, and commerce. According to the report, "the
vast majority of those surveyed agreed that 'this cathedral reaches out
beyond the Church of England', or that it was 'a "hub" to engage the life
of the wider community."[4] Moreover, the majority of non-churchgoers
agreed that the cathedral contributes to the community and regarded it
as relevant to their daily lives. The vast majority of those surveyed (87 per
cent) agreed that cathedrals are symbols of local identity, a sentiment that
was even stronger amongst those who identified as "non religious" (90 per
cent). Once again, this finding is intuitively convincing: cathedrals have
multiple stakeholders reaching far beyond the confines of the Church of
England and are often crucial to the civic life, history, and economy of
their region.

The second finding of the report "Spiritual Capital" I should like to
highlight concerns the cathedral as a place of spirituality. Until relatively
recently, research into cathedrals made a distinction between pilgrim
visitors and tourist visitors. "Spiritual Capital" challenges this neat
distinction.[5] The local survey of around 1,400 people familiar with one
of six cathedrals—Canterbury, Durham, Lichfield, Leicester, Manchester,
and Wells—showed that 30 per cent of people agreed with the statement,
"I come here to appreciate the history and architecture of the cathedral,
not for any religious/sacred experience." These respondents therefore
identify as what the report calls "secular tourists". Within this group of
"secular tourists", the survey revealed the following:

84% of this group still agreed or strongly agreed with the
idea that they got a sense of the sacred from the cathedral
building; 79% that they got a sense of the sacred from the
cathedral music; and 56% agreed or strongly agreed that
they experienced God through the calm and the quiet of
the cathedral space.[6]

The cathedral is therefore a place that provokes a sense of the sacred and
transcendent, even amongst those whose motives for visiting a cathedral
lie elsewhere.

In this chapter, I will use these findings—the "bridging" social capital
of cathedrals and their significance for provoking a sense of the sacred
and transcendent—to examine theologically and philosophically why
cathedrals are significant in our religious and social landscape. What are
the deeper roots of cathedral growth? First, I will argue that the theology
of the cathedral is associated with the visible unity of the Church. Because
the cathedral witnesses first and foremost to the one body of Christ as the
mother church of the diocese under the oversight of the bishop, it can also
foster the unity of a local, national, or even global community. Secondly,
I will argue that cathedrals, because of their symbolic significance and
sacramental life, penetrate the thick buffers of the individual self that
characterize the modern person so as to situate that person within a
much wider cosmic narrative of creation and salvation. The penetration
of the sacred into the lives of modern people is an important aspect of
cathedrals' enduring appeal and importance.

THE THEOLOGY OF THE CATHEDRAL: UNITY OF CHURCH AND COMMUNITY

A theology of the cathedral belongs primarily within the sphere of
ecclesiology—the study of the nature and mission of the Church. I will
therefore begin with a basic outline of those aspects of ecclesiology relevant
to a theological understanding of the cathedral.

Scripturally, we trace the beginning of the Church as the Spirit-filled body of Christ to two texts: John 20. 22 when Jesus breathes the Holy Spirit onto his disciples; and Acts 2, the first Pentecost, when the Spirit descends on the followers of Christ in Jerusalem. What is brought to birth at that first Pentecost is not simply a local church of Jerusalem, but the Church catholic. Catholic in what sense? The Church which is brought to birth at the first Pentecost is both local—the church of Jerusalem—but also catholic in the sense that, as well as being one, *there is nowhere it does not belong.* This aspect of ecclesiology is very important: Christianity is not for anyone in particular. It is not for a particular racial group, a particular cultural group, an intellectual elite, or a certain generation. Acts 2 emphasizes the sheer cultural and linguistic diversity of the group gathered in Jerusalem at the moment the Spirit descends. St Paul's letters make clear that in Christ all are one, for there is no Jew and Gentile, male and female, slave and free. The books that form the New Testament are the first books in antiquity which are gathered for a universal readership rather than a particular cultural, racial, or intellectual group. Ephesians 1 makes clear that Christ is "the head over all things for the church, which is his body, the fullness of him who fills all in all." From the very inception of the faith and the body of Christ into which we are grafted by baptism, there is no domain in which the message and presence of Christ does not belong. In absolute terms, there is no secular and neutral domain which it is not the Church's responsibility to inhabit in a gracious and benevolent form, carrying with it the presence of the risen Christ. Realizing that we are part of the catholic Church—catholic at least in the sense that the Church is one and belongs everywhere—should make Christians absolutely resistant to the view that there is any aspect of creation and human society beyond the reach of God's Word. Given Colossians 1. 16—"for in him all things in heaven and on earth were created, things visible and invisible, whether thrones or dominions or rulers or powers—all things have been created through him and for him"—how could it be otherwise?

Christianity's universality and particularity presented a number of challenges very early in its history. The period in which most of the New Testament texts were written was a time when the return of Christ was thought to be imminent. Those with teaching authority were the original witnesses of Jesus' earthly ministry or, by dint of his extraordinary conversion and missionary zeal, St Paul. As those first witnesses began to die out, a crisis of authority ensued. Who could now teach within the Church? How was the continuity of that teaching with the apostolic witness to be maintained? The answer: through the physical laying on of hands and the appointment of a new generation of overseers who were connected to the previous generation of overseers. The episcopate therefore answers the question concerning how the unity of the Church *across time* is to be maintained. This is why the Anglican, Orthodox, and Roman Catholic Churches preserve the *historic* episcopate—the episcopate extending back through time via the laying on of hands—to preserve and make visible the unity of the Church across time. The unity of the Church across time refers to the inseparability of the Church in the present age from the Church of the apostles and the oecumenical councils of the first six centuries. In other words, the Church established by Christ upon the rock of Peter is one and the same Church of which we are members today.

The early Church also faced another challenge. Because Christianity is both particular and universal, it traversed cultural boundaries very quickly. Initially, it seemed to unite both Hellenistic and Hebraic cultures as it spread across the Mediterranean. St Paul's letters are in large part focused on the question of how one preserves the unity of the Church's witness in the face of ever-increasing cultural diversity and geographical spread. In the second century a response to this question was to appoint overseers with a shepherding and teaching office which was focused particularly on the building up of the one body of Christ. But the unity of the Church in this kind of context cannot rest on everyone agreeing to a set of very particular propositions. Even grounding the unity of the Church on the proclamation of scripture is problematic because interpretations of scripture vary. The history of continual splits in the Protestant churches bears witness to this. The unity of the Church is a gift of the Spirit rather than something of our own making. Because we are physical, corporeal beings who do not exist only in the realm of ideas and propositions, the unity of the Church has to be made *visible*. We must be able to *see* that unity in such a way that it transcends the opinions and predilections of individuals, or a particular locale, generation, or culture. For Roman Catholics, the unity of the Church is most particularly visible in the Pope.

For Anglicans and Orthodox, the unity of the Church is made visible in the bishop and, at the provincial level, by the episcopal primus or Patriarch.

One of the most important aspects of episcopal ministry, therefore, concerns the protection (an important aspect of shepherding) of the unity of the Church in obedience to Christ's prayer and St Paul's teaching (John 17. 20–24; 1 Corinthians 12. 12–31). The cathedral, in being first and foremost the seat or *cathedra* of the bishop, shares in the ministry of gathering and unifying the Church in a visible fashion. The cathedral is the place from which the bishop oversees and teaches—it is the platform from which the bishop can address God's people and minister to their needs. Within Anglican polity, the bishop has no formal jurisdiction within his or her cathedral. Governance lies principally with the autonomous dean and chapter, assisted by the College of Canons and overseen by a representative Cathedral Council. The cathedral is, therefore, a *gift* to the bishop from the dean and chapter on behalf of the diocese. The bishop does not possess the cathedral by canonical or juridical right. The people of God invite the bishop's oversight in the gift of the cathedral from which he or she sends and leads as a labourer in the vineyard.

In the ministry of the bishop in the cathedral, three potent and visible signs of the unity of the Church coalesce: the bishop ministering the sacraments of baptism and Eucharist within the mother church of the diocese. That unity is made most visible at the Easter vigil when the bishop baptizes, confirms, and presides at the Eucharist within her cathedral on the day of resurrection. It is also made visible as the bishop presides at ordinations because all clergy share his or her cure of souls according to the Spirit's direction through God's people. The crucial point, however, is the threefold *visible* unity of the Church: the bishop in her cathedral presiding at the Eucharist.

The ministry of cathedrals as places of gathering and unity is founded upon their position within the Church as a visible sign of the unity of the body of Christ. This theology of the cathedral is the basis of the wider role of cathedrals in fostering and *making visible* a local, national, or global unity.[7] Today's cathedrals have numerous stakeholders and are the locus for countless gatherings of civic and cultural importance: funerals of important public figures, the remembrance of war or local tragedy, thanksgiving for civic and commercial success, public debate, and cultural celebration. In my own cathedral, Durham, we host—on consecutive days—a service for the annual Durham Miners' Gala and a service for the Courts of Justice. Both are attended by around a thousand people. Both are politically potent symbols of, respectively, trade unionism and industry, and the Queen's peace preserved by the rule of law. The Bishop presides at both and a sermon is preached. The gathering and unifying ministry of the cathedral is part of the bishop's oversight of all people and the furtherance of unity and peace. As such, the cathedral realizes the catholic nature of the Church because it reaches out and gathers all people across civic society, convinced that there is no place in which Christian proclamation does not belong. But the cathedral does not exercise this ministry by being neutral or "all things to all people", but by welcoming everyone as a child of God to whom the grace of Christ is offered. Just as the New Testament church traversed boundaries of race, gender, social status, and culture, so the cathedral traverses boundaries of sacred and secular, public and private, because all are one in Christ. The gathering and unifying ministry of cathedrals is not grounded in a political, cultural, or economic consensus, but in the prayer of Christ that God's people might be one as he and the Father are one. Of course, our unity as a Church and our unity as civic communities is partial and compromised at best, but the cathedral witnesses to the dawning Kingdom of God when all shall be perfectly one in Christ.

The ministry of gathering to become a visible sign of unity can be related to an Anglican sensibility focused on the so-called *via media*. The *via media* is frequently understood as a love of balance, restraint, moderation, and measure which treads a middle way between the extremes of Protestantism and Catholicism. It is as if the Church of England and other Anglican Provinces are uniquely able to discern the narrow path between two heresies. This "middle way" apparently makes the Church of England and its cathedrals uniquely placed to appeal to anyone and everyone in civic society. As Edmund Newey has shown, there is another understanding of the *via media* that is more to do with catholicity or wholeness of the kind proposed in the first part of this chapter.[8] In an Easter sermon preached in 1609, around the time he was translated from the See of Chichester to the See of Ely, Launcelot Andrewes described the Church of England's "middle way". Christ is a mediator not by compromise, but by *comprehension*; the Church continues that comprehensive ministry, a ministry which belongs everywhere. The church historian Gregory Dodds writes:

> Andrewes's *via media* rhetoric was not simply referring to a moderate middle space. Like Erasmus, Andrewes defines moderation and the *via media* as a "middle" trajectory between God and man, earth and heaven. This vertical *via media* helped shape his conception of the horizontal *via media* found on this earth. For Erasmus and Andrewes, the middle way was a middle pathway on which human beings made progress from earthly issues to heavenly salvation.[9]

In other words, the *via media* is as much about heaven meeting earth as it is about doctrinal moderation. And where does heaven meet earth salvifically, other than in the Word incarnate? So the Church is a *via media* in the sense that it shares in the life of Christ at the joining of heaven and earth and the gathering into unity of divine and human natures.

Here we find a very traditional and ancient view of unity and hierarchy in which the cathedral has a central place. Today, we tend to think of hierarchy as "top down". For example, the Queen stands at the top of our political hierarchy with the commoners at the bottom. The Queen has many layers between her and the commoners. This is the kind of hierarchy that liberal modernity dislikes. We would rather have a more democratic and levelled social order, even if that means the eradication of all significant difference between social roles and vocations. But for ancient and mediaeval thinkers, hierarchy was understood differently. It was more "middle out" than "top down".[10] The Church was, of course, seen as hierarchical in the sense that each "member" had his or her place within the body with Christ as the head. Christ was understood as head of the Church because he gathered the body into a unity and was its centre. Crucially, Christ was understood as equally present to every point in the hierarchy of the Church, whether that point appeared distant from, or close to, the centre. A good visual and practical expression of the importance of the centre can be found in labyrinths which are now commonly found in cathedrals. Unlike a maze, which is designed to lose a person and in which no turning is any more preferable than any other, a labyrinth is a journey in which the pilgrim is drawn to an end or goal. When the pilgrim seems to be near to the centre of the labyrinth, suddenly it throws her to the edge. When at the edge, the pilgrim thinks that she is far from the end of the journey, but is suddenly taken directly to the centre. The centre is, as it were, as close to the paths at the edge as it is to the path near the middle.

The Church, therefore, is a *via media* because it has a centre that gathers everything to itself and comprehends the whole. The diocese has the particular centre of its ministry—not a geographical but a theological centre—in the cathedral and the figure of the bishop who teaches and shepherds from the *cathedra*. The cathedral is an expression of the Anglican *via media* in which the middle is Christ, not in terms of compromise but in terms of *comprehension*, for Christ "fills all in all" (Ephesians 1. 23). The cathedral needs to be comprehensive in its ministry, not compromising in its ministry, being equally present to every part of the hierarchy of Christ's body, the Church. This does not mean that the cathedral must offer every kind of worship or event imaginable. Indeed, there is a strong argument that the cathedral should not try to replicate in one church everything that goes on in parishes because that will simply repeat differences and fragmentation. Rather, the cathedral must retain a comprehension of the deep tradition of Christian liturgy and spirituality that lies at the root of every particular example of Christian life and practice in the contemporary church.

The cathedral exercises this ministry of gathering and unifying within the context of a secular world that does not itself provide a unifying "middle". Contemporary society is radically de-centred in the sense of having no focus beyond the local shopping centre. When bombs explode on our streets, a member of the Royal Family dies, a nation remembers its war dead, or a national society or charity wants to celebrate the anniversary of its founding, we default to a more substantial and enduring "middle", the cathedral, which, because of its Christian proclamation, provides an expression of unity and hope that exceeds the chaotic pluralities of modern society. It is a genuine *via media*, lying comprehensively *in the middle* of public and private, sacred and secular, heaven and earth. This is why cathedrals provide such vital "bridging" social capital, but a social capital that is founded upon the ministry of making visible the unity and catholicity of the Church.

Another important aspect of this gathering ministry of unification can be seen in an essay by the Catholic philosopher Charles Taylor, who points out that the Reformation involved an attempt to bring all members of the Church up to the highest standards of the Christian gospel.[11] In other words, there was an attempt to overcome a distinction between clergy and the religious on the one hand, and other Christians on the other. In ancient and mediaeval Christianity there were a variety of vocations which included differing calls to perfection and different forms of life. The Reformers took the view, later adopted by Roman Catholics at the Counter-Reformation, that this was hierarchical religious elitism which encouraged certain people—the strict religious, for example—to be prideful or to seek power or wealth. From the fifteenth century, there were only two categories: the saved and the damned. All saved Christians must be "one hundred per cent": you are either in or you are out. The unintended consequence of this, according to Taylor, was the creation of a secular domain, the world lying outside the walls of the church or cathedral, the world of those who are "out" rather than "in". Taylor writes:

> The Reformation also tended to delegitimate the distinction between fully committed believers and other, less devoted ones. As against a view of the church in which people operating at many different "speeds" coexisted with religious "virtuosi", to use Max Weber's term, on one end, and ordinary intermittent practitioners, on the other, all Christians were expected to be fully committed.[12]

Anglicans have a particular sensitivity to the complex nature of human religiosity. The majority of people are neither straightforwardly "in" or "out". Their sense of God, their need of the Church, and their commitment to the faith ebb and flow. People journey at different speeds and most inhabit the penumbra of Christianity. This is why it is problematic to categorize visitors to cathedrals as either tourists or pilgrims. Reading the prayers which people leave behind or looking at the number of candles lit by visitors suggests that the experience deep in people's souls is much more complex than the binary "believer vs unbeliever" might indicate. Even a convinced "tourist visitor" may find herself becoming just a little porous to the Christian story as she enters the beating heart of a living cathedral. So it may be that the secular realm of devout unbelievers forming the core of the modern UK is too simplistic and rather part of a new atheist fantasy. The enduring popularity of cathedrals and their ability to gather and make visible a unity beyond mere individual preference points to an alternative and more complex religious landscape.

Having examined the corporate and communal importance of the ministry of cathedrals, I now turn to the individual. The second finding of the report "Spiritual Capital" highlighted above concerns the importance of cathedrals as places of spiritual significance and discovery, even amongst visitors who regard their motivations as historical and cultural rather than religious. Why does the spiritual significance of cathedrals persist, even amongst those individuals who do not self-identify as Christian or even religious?

THE CATHEDRAL AND THE MODERN SELF

The cultural and religious circumstances in which our great Romanesque and Gothic mediaeval cathedrals were built is almost unimaginable to the modern mind. The world of the Middle Ages featured a deep theological imagination in which all things, both in nature and human culture, were oriented towards a transcendent God who was the mysterious beginning and end of all things. The secular was simply that which contrasted with the *saecula saeculorum*: the secular was the age which would pass away, roughly equivalent to the human lifespan in Roman antiquity. It was distinguished from the ages of ages, the Kingdom of God, which would endure for eternity. The twenty-first-century cathedral operates within a different secular age which began to emerge around the sixteenth century. The standard secularization thesis is known as "subtraction" and the story goes something like this. In the fifteenth and sixteenth centuries, the Wars of Religion and the Reformation led to violent religious conflict throughout Europe. In an attempt to resolve such conflicts, appeals were made to non-religious criteria which were apparently neutral. So begins the rolling back or "subtraction" of the Christian theological imagination in the face of philosophical rationalism and the rise of modern natural science. Whereas in the Middle Ages philosophy had been the handmaid of theology, philosophy now turned to scrutinize theology according to different standards of reason and apparently found it wanting. The rolling back or subtraction of the Christian imagination and cosmology apparently left behind the cool, clean air of indifferent and independent rationalism to which any free human being has access simply by virtue of his innate rational powers. We were left with a neutral public sphere dominated by "reason" (understood in a particular way) and religion became a matter of private and personal preference. At the same time, reason was sundered from faith. So secularization is simply about the subtraction or removal of religious imagination to reveal something more neutral and peaceful.

As a number of commentators point out, notably Charles Taylor and the Anglican theologian John Milbank, the situation is much more complex.[13] They argue that the demise of the Christian theological imagination—what the German sociologist Max Weber called "the disenchantment of the world"—does not reveal the secular as a neutral sphere. The secular is a positive construction with its own particular brand of rationality and its own cosmology. It is, as Milbank would put it, a kind of ersatz theology in which other kinds of "ultimate concern" come to take the place of theological transcendence. In the end, Milbank points to secularism's parasitic relationship to religion and theology; he describes secularism as a Christian heresy. Witness Alain de Botton's proposal to build a Temple of Atheism in London or A. C. Grayling's *The Good Book: A Secular Bible*, the most blatant piece of asset stripping one could imagine. These are, in different ways, parasitic on a theological perspective on humanity and the world.

The secular is not a neutral sphere devoid of theology and religious significance. It has its own account of "ultimate commitments", however deracinated that account might often appear to be. It is a sphere in which the modern cathedral finds itself as the embodiment of a more perennial reason and truth expressed in ritual, prayer and teaching. Alongside the process of secularization, Taylor discerns a shifting conception of the human person. His extensive work in philosophical anthropology leads him to make a distinction between what he calls the ancient and mediaeval "porous self" and the modern "buffered self".[14] The mediaeval porous self was open to the meanings and powers inherent in all created things including the blessed sacrament, relics, and other sacred objects. The porous self was open to possession by other powers, whether they be evil spirits or the Holy Spirit. This made the porous self potentially vulnerable. It was understood as part of a cosmic drama and pattern of meaning in which self-determination was not absolute. When the mediaeval craftsman helped to create a great cathedral, the building was more than just beautiful and impressive. It was more than just an achievement of human skill and testimony to human munificence. It was a building of enormous power which was somehow more than the power of its manufacturers and architects. It was, in a sense that is more than merely figurative, "alive"; it had the power to form human selves because those selves were porous and susceptible to cosmic powers, including the power of a cathedral. Add a shrine at the heart of a cathedral—an Alban or a Cuthbert—and pilgrims had a very strong sense of not being autonomous and self-determining, but part of a pattern of mysterious meanings and interwoven lives past and present, all pointing towards God who is both utterly transcendent but also closer to us than our own breathing.

By contrast, Taylor describes the modern self as "buffered". The advent of the buffered self was not simply the result of subtracting mediaeval beliefs and superstitions; it was the positive construction of a different kind of self-identity and self-understanding. According to Taylor's description of the modern buffered self, there is a strong boundary between a mental or psychic "me", somewhere inside my body but independent of my body, and the outside world. The buffered self is much more self-determined and therefore fundamentally individual, separate from the created and natural order, inhabiting a realm we call "cultural". Things like trees, landscapes, or cathedrals no longer have any intrinsic meaning, but only the meaning given to them by modern buffered selves which stand over and against them. Taylor writes:

> the buffered self can form the ambition of disengaging
> from whatever is beyond the boundary, and of giving its

own autonomous order to its life. The absence of fear can
be not just enjoyed, but becomes an opportunity for self-
control or self-direction.[15]

A good example of the buffered self can be found in our ability to
disconnect ourselves even from our bodies. Imagine you are worried
you have depression. You go to the doctor and she tells you that it is just
a hormone imbalance or a problem with certain neural receptors. That is
good because you can distance yourself from these physical symptoms: "It's
not me, it's the hormones or the neurons." In other words, there is an "I"
even behind my body and I can, to some extent, distinguish that "I" and
buffer it, not only from the outside world, but even from my own body.

   Taylor is not proposing a return to the porous self in a fit of nostalgia,
even if such a thing were remotely possible. To be a Christian, however,
requires a degree of porosity. It requires a sense that reality is more than
a buffered, autonomous self that stands over and against other selves
and things. It requires a porosity to powers beyond oneself, particularly
the power and providence of God the Holy Spirit. It also suggests that
created, physical things are not merely objects for our manipulation or
exploitation, but have an intrinsic meaning and power in forming who
we are. In other words, Christians are open to, and intimately part of, the
sacramental power of creation. The sacramental theology even of John
Calvin would see the self as porous to the power of humble bread, wine,
water, and oil in the sacraments of baptism and the Eucharist.

   Visitors to cathedrals are brought into an environment in which the self
can become a little more porous. The cathedral, because of its immensity,
beauty, and history, because it is saturated with symbol and meaning,
because it is warm with the prayers of many generations and therefore
open to powers beyond the self, penetrates the buffers of self-determination
and autonomy. We might put this another way. The modern buffered self,
standing over and against the outside world, tends to think that Christianity
is a matter of the individual's assent to a set of propositions or even the
choosing of a certain form of life. But the Christian tradition, exemplified
in Augustine of Hippo's *Confessions*, suggests something rather different:
it is not that the self assents to, or seizes, some external proposition, fact,
or being. Rather, the self is *seized by* something that is not entirely within

its control. The self is porous to a power that is not its own. God finds us, we do not find God. To be grasped, rather than to grasp, demands a certain kind of porosity and a sense that we are not masters of meaning or truth. The world is not limited to what I perceive of it; the depth of being and meaning infinitely exceeds the mere appearances of things. So while many visitors will come to our cathedrals thinking, "What can I get from this visit by way of interesting history, a pleasing sense of beauty, or a tea towel?", there may be a nagging sense that the inner self has been opened just a crack in such a way that the visitor is grasped by something—a real power—beyond themselves, an echo of a pre-modern world of cosmic drama and meaning. Maybe that is why even so-called "tourist visitors" light candles and leave prayers. The power of the cathedral to penetrate the autonomy and self-determination of the modern self (an autonomy which we too often mistake for freedom) perhaps lies behind the findings of reports such as "Spiritual Capital" that visitors of all kinds find them to be spiritually significant in such a way that tourist visitors become pilgrims in their encounter with the cathedral. It takes something like a cathedral to make one realize, even for a split second, that one's immediate circumstances are ultimately fragile and contingent.

CONCLUSION

The success of today's cathedrals—at least, their ability to resist the apparent decline in church attendance and extend the scope of their ministry—can be attributed to a number of obvious factors: professional music, sufficient clergy to maintain consistently high quality liturgy and preaching, continuous investment in buildings and exhibition spaces, professionalized visitor services and education departments, material riches in the form of libraries and treasures, a variety of worship, and the resources to offer services and events throughout the week. This essay has attempted to delve behind some of these (obviously true) explanations to examine theologically why we have cathedrals in the first place and how they fit within the current religious and cultural landscape.

Taking a longer historical view, however, one factor remains frequently overlooked: the recovery in the nineteenth century of the roots of cathedral ministry in monastic life. Prior to the Reform Act of 1832, cathedrals were in a parlous state with bloated chapters, deans who were rarely in residence, and buildings in a state of advanced decay. During the nineteenth century, governance was reformed and a programme of restoration undertaken to make cathedrals fit for public worship once again. Today the more diligent care of cathedral fabric continues, but at considerable cost: many cathedrals invest very heavily in buildings and visitor services and their fabric has never been in such good condition. In paying for the care and ambitious development of their buildings, cathedrals push their finances to the very limit—and in some cases beyond. One further consequence of these nineteenth century governance reforms was the renewal of a vital aspect of cathedral life: its praying heart. I have argued that the cathedral lies at the middle of Church and community, a *via media* and a visible sign of gathered unity. The cathedral is a theological and spiritual centre for the diocese and civic society. The cathedral itself, however, has a middle: the daily round of morning and evening prayer overseen by the cathedral chapter on behalf of the bishop, diocese, and people. This is an echo of the monastic tradition that lies explicitly behind some of our mediaeval monastic cathedrals (Canterbury, Durham, Rochester, Ely, Lichfield, Norwich, Worcester) and implicitly behind other cathedrals in their structures and patterns of worship. Indeed, the report "Spiritual Capital" points out that the Benedictine pattern of prayer and the ministry of welcome continues to influence the way in which cathedrals perceive their life and mission today.[16]

Cathedrals have been very successful in exploiting their position as visible signs of ecclesial and civic unity as well as the power of their architecture, history, and material treasures to penetrate the modern sense of spiritual alienation, self-determination, and autonomy. Within a dogmatic secular culture that regards religion as a private matter of weird superstition, this is a remarkable achievement of considerable missional significance for sustaining the Church's public credibility and influence. Without a doubt, the greatest challenge facing cathedrals today is financial. Many are in long-term financial crisis because of their laudable ambition and the very significant demands and expectations placed upon them by local communities, multiple stakeholders, and the wider church. Cathedrals seem to be more popular than ever, but no one has yet devised a compelling and sustainable plan to pay for them. Whilst many compete for heritage grants, they receive no government funding. Beyond the provision of three clergy stipends, only some cathedrals—generally those outside significant tourist destinations—receive a modest central church grant. Finding a source of funding that does not compromise cathedrals' monastic heritage, their ministry as a visible sign of ecclesial and civic unity, and the autonomy of their governance remains a very significant challenge.

Meanwhile, further opportunities will arise for cathedrals as they consolidate their exploitation of material and spiritual assets. Most particularly, the further development of cathedrals as centres of learning and public debate—developed very successfully in recent years by St Paul's and Westminster Abbey—is one obvious area for exploration. So too is the continual development of the missional relationship between the cathedral, the bishop and parishes. Any future growth, however, must continue to be rooted in the praying heart of the cathedral, for this is where the source of spiritual capital has been found in the gradual revival and continued success of cathedral ministry over recent generations.

NOTES

1. "Cathedral Statistics 2015" (Church of England Research and Statistics, 2016), available at <https://www.churchofengland.org/media/2859050/2015_cathedral_statistics.pdf> (accessed 11 November 2016).

2. "Spiritual Capital: The Present and Future of English Cathedrals"(Theos and The Grubb Institute, 2012), available at <http://www.theosthinktank.co.uk/publications/2012/10/12/spiritual-capital-the-present-and-future-of-english-cathedrals> (accessed 11 November 2016). "Spiritual Capital" is based on a national survey of 1,700 adults commissioned for the project and a local survey of 1,933 adults who were asked their opinions of one of six Church of England cathedrals with which they were familiar: Canterbury, Durham, Lichfield, Leicester, Manchester, and Wells. There was a further set of 257 in-depth qualitative interviews of people working in and with these six cathedrals.

3. "Spiritual Capital", p. 12.

4. "Spiritual Capital", p. 12.

5. "Spiritual Capital", p.14.

6. "Spiritual Capital", p.18.

7. All cathedrals exercise a ministry of gathering the local community. In addition, St Paul's Cathedral has a particular role in gathering the nation and Canterbury has a particular role as a focus for the unity of the global Anglican Communion.

8. See Edmund Newey, "The Covenant and the *Via Media*: Compatible or Contradictory Notions of Anglicanism?" in Benjamin Guyer (ed.), *Pro Communione: Theological Essays on the Anglican Covenant* (Pickwick Publications, 2012).

9. Gregory D. Dodds, *Exploiting Erasmus: The Erasmian Legacy and Religious Change in Early Modern England* (Toronto University Press, 2009), p. 189, quoted in Newey, "The Covenant and the *Via Media*", p. 56.

10. One of the last attempts to preserve this sense of hierarchy can be found in Nicholas of Cusa, *The Catholic Concordance (De concordantia catholica)*, trans. Paul E. Sigmund (Cambridge University Press, 1991), written in 1433. For example, Book 1 paragraph 10: "Thus I think of the Word from above as like a magnetic stone the power of which extends through everything down to the lowest being. Its infinite power is not lacking down through the ranks, but there is a marvellous order of interconnection among finite and limited creatures."

11. Charles Taylor, "The Future of the Religious Past" in idem., *Dilemmas and Connections: Selected Essays* (Harvard University Press, 2011), pp. 214–286.

12. Taylor, *Dilemmas and Connections*, p. 215. Interestingly, Taylor argues that New Atheism follows the same pattern of insisting that everyone is essentially the same—atheist rather than religious believer.

13. John Milbank, *Theology and Social Theory: Beyond Secular Reason*, 2nd edition (Blackwell, 2006); Charles Taylor, *A Secular Age* (The Belknap Press of Harvard University Press, 2007).

14. See Taylor, *A Secular Age*, pp. 37–42. For a succinct explanation of this distinction, see Charles Taylor, "Buffered and Porous Selves": <http://blogs.ssrc.org/tif/2008/09/02/buffered-and-porous-selves/comment-page-1/> (accessed 17 September 2016).

15. Taylor, "Buffered and Porous Selves" (accessed 25 April 2014).

16. "Spiritual Capital", pp. 32–33.

3.   ENCOURAGING EXCELLENCE

Jennie Page

"I did not join the Church of England to be a building manager," was the exasperated assertion of the eminent dean of an ancient cathedral, now long retired, when confronted, some twenty-five years ago, with the need to answer for an aspect of the care of his cathedral's fabric. Yet responsibility for the physical fabric of worship buildings has been part of the role of the dean and chapter of a cathedral, as it has of every parish incumbent, for about a thousand years: it comes with the job. What was new on this occasion was the recent enactment of the Care of Cathedrals Measure 1990, which for the first time imposed unavoidable constraints for the dean on the previously unfettered exercise of the role. This, perhaps, was what made the responsibility feel more onerous and less in keeping with his vocation.

This chapter reviews the history behind the Measure, and some aspects of the operation since then of the bodies it created—the Cathedrals Fabric Commission for England and the individual cathedral Fabric Advisory Committees. It is written by one who served ten years on the Commission (2006–16) and has continuing roles on two such committees, but all the views expressed are personal and not to be held to the account of any of those bodies.

HISTORIC BACKGROUND

The framework of controls over the care of the fabric of the cathedrals of the Church of England is unique, as is so much about the cathedrals, for reasons to be found in the early history of the Christian church in England. Differences established then were perpetuated at the time of the Reformation and confirmed when cathedrals, abolished in the Commonwealth, were, apparently without much consideration, re-introduced with their governance unchanged, on the Restoration. As Christopher Haigh has said, we have cathedrals because no-one successfully decided not to have them,[1] and we have an inherited governance structure which has left cathedrals—including cathedrals only consecrated in the late nineteenth and early twentieth centuries—free from the legal controls which have applied for around a thousand years to physical works to parochial churches. Parish clergy were obliged from early days to petition the bishop's legal official, the chancellor of the diocese, for a faculty to carry out building works, thus acknowledging episcopal oversight of the provision of appropriate fittings and facilities for public worship. The bishop's prior authority has not been required for comparable works in the cathedral, the seat of episcopal power. This reflects the origin of the cathedral as the bishop's household church under his direct control. That control was substantially weakened in the early mediaeval period by the delegation of powers to the predecessors of the dean and chapter, who ran the diocesan seat while the bishop pursued other interests—frequently in support of the monarch—elsewhere. Thus were created the formal distance and potential tension between bishop and cathedral which still exist. So the dean and chapter's freedom from oversight in respect of the care of the building survived throughout the early modern period.

It was only when secular interest in historic monuments became more powerful, towards the end of the nineteenth century, that this total absence of control became an obvious rather than ignored anomaly. By 1913 some members of the House of Lords were persuaded that cathedrals should at least be given the protection of state oversight and potential ownership.

> The cathedrals, as I understand, are the absolute property
> for the time being of the dean and chapter, and they can,

as regards the fabric, do what they please. I should be most sorry if I were thought to imply that deans and chapters are not most scrupulous in the exercise of the sacred trust which is in their hands. I know how particular they are in appointing special architects for the fabrics entrusted to their charge, and what enormous and reverent care they devote to the custody of these buildings. But there are as great differences between architects as there are between theologians, and the possession of a special architect does not save your cathedral from injury which is in some cases almost irreparable. Therefore I myself would like nothing better than to see our cathedrals—which, after all, are the most glorious national monuments we possess, excelling our palaces and our castles—put into the list of scheduled monuments, so that it would be impossible to touch them without the consent of the State as advised by an Ancient Monuments Board.[2]

This attempt to capture the cathedral was unsuccessful, not so much owing to parliamentary faith in the excellence of deans and chapters as because the passage of legislation affecting church matters was thought too time-consuming.[3] All ecclesiastical buildings in use for worship were specifically excluded from the terms of the Ancient Monuments Consolidation and Amendment Act 1913 under what we know to this day as ecclesiastical exemption. (However, structures within the precincts of a cathedral may be designated as scheduled ancient monuments and the appropriate protective legislation does apply to these.) Alongside perpetuation of the mediaeval faculty system for parochial churches, cathedrals were permitted to retain their right to operate without intervention. This was not universally thought to be a good thing and some cathedrals, in subsequent years, voluntarily provided themselves with local committees of persons able to provide advice about the architectural and archaeological importance of the buildings. In the late 1940s, a central Cathedrals Advisory Committee of experts in the care of ancient buildings was created, from which advice could be sought by those cathedral authorities who wanted assistance. Complaints by both sides were being made by 1967,[4] but no changes were made until the committee, with widened membership, became permanent as the Cathedrals Advisory Commission (CAC) of General Synod in 1981. But even with this encouragement to respect its relevance, various chapters failed to bind themselves to consult the CAC, demonstrating cathedrals' continuing lack of enthusiasm for the system and, perhaps, for any intervention in the sole rights of deans and chapters. By 1982, a church investigatory body received a CAC claim that the system was not working, and commented, "Major alterations to the fabric made by certain chapters (and in some cases the proposed disposal of treasures) have caused much public disquiet at various times during the last fifty years."[5]

Such disquiet was public because cathedrals had emerged during the 1950s to 1970s from a comparative backwater into general awareness, owing to their increasing role in local and international tourism and to the "general inclination to give an enhanced priority to the preservation of national cultural treasures"[6] which contributed to the development of the heritage industry. There was increasing publicity for various fundraising efforts for significant expenditure on necessary works (the largest at that time being £2 million to stop the collapse of York Minster, then sometimes known as "the crumbling cathedral"). As early as 1967 the suggestion of public support for the 28 "ancient cathedrals" was raised in Parliament. Lord Jellicoe, the proponent, added:

> As a "quid pro quo" the Church might possibly be asked voluntarily to agree to submit its great cathedrals to the same sort (I do not say the same, but the same sort) of planning disciplines as govern our secular buildings.[7]

The deal hypothecated here in respect of cathedrals was not taken up but began to be worked out in the following decade in respect of churches. The Agreement for State Aid for Churches in Use, endorsed by General Synod in 1977, noted:

> It is recognised that these are matters for the Church of England and the Consistory Courts, but the Government would welcome any modifications [in the faculty system] which could help to allay any disquiet on the part of

local authorities and the general public about the present arrangements.[8]

The consequent review by the Faculty Jurisdiction Commission, published in 1984 as *The Continuing Care of Churches and Cathedrals*, fulfilled this function, thus securing the continuation of state aid for churches, and also laid the groundwork for the changes which would permit the creation of the first cathedrals grants scheme. It did so by accepting that it was essential "to satisfy the requirements of public accountability" to have a statutory system for cathedrals whereby consultation by chapters was mandatory, and advice was binding. In a drinking-in-the-last-chance-saloon paragraph, the Commission warned that "it only needs one action by a chapter against the advice of the CAC to cause a public outcry which might well lead to legislation which would seriously circumscribe the responsibilities of chapters ... [I]t seems to us that the cathedrals will themselves benefit in the long run by having a carefully worked out system which will afford a chapter the opportunity of appealing against the advice of the CAC."[9]

BIRTH OF THE CATHEDRALS FABRIC COMMISSION FOR ENGLAND

General Synod accepted the recommended changes but threw out the first attempt at a Measure to implement them. The cathedral lobby resisted the desire of the amenity societies and others to apply the full secular planning and heritage protections, and, in face of potential stalemate and as an encouragement to the Church to implement reform, government agreed in October 1986 that existing ecclesiastical exemptions (principally from listed building consent) would remain and that the tempting possibility of cathedral grants which was held out would not be time-limited. Following detailed review by a Revision Committee of General Synod, much negotiation between parties with conflicting views, and changes to the draft Measure, under the Care of Cathedrals Measure

1990 the new system was introduced in 1991. Shortly afterwards, an English Heritage-administered cathedral grants scheme began: funded solely by public money for most of its nineteen years' existence, the scheme had the Wolfson Foundation as a partner in later years. £52 million was distributed.

Statutory enforcement provisions were added in 1994 and, with only minor subsequent amendments in 2005 and consolidation in 2011, this legislative system continues. Its key components are the statutory Cathedrals Fabric Commission for England (CFCE), and an individual Fabric Advisory Committee (FAC) for each cathedral, from one or other of which a chapter must obtain approval before undertaking certain works to the cathedral, its contents, or its setting. In exercising their statutory roles both the CFCE and the FACs must have regard to the fact that the cathedral is "the seat of the bishop and the centre of worship and mission".[10] This provision, taken together with the composition of the CFCE (see below), is designed to ensure that, while the heritage value of a cathedral is taken seriously, persuasive arguments from the active life of the cathedral can justify heritage loss.[11] The CFCE can call in decisions on projects which would otherwise be decided by an FAC if it considers their impact to be significant. In addition, the CFCE is empowered to offer advice to cathedrals: this it does generally through policy guidance, conferences, and training days, and specifically in response to requests for schemes under development. It supports the individual FACs with advice and contributes to the selection of members of each FAC. There is provision (to date untested) for appeal by the applicant from a CFCE decision to a special Commission of Review, consisting of the Dean of Arches, an appointee of the Archbishops and an appointee of the Secretary of State.

The Measure did not represent a defeat for the cathedrals. CFCE members (other than the Chair and vice-chair, a bishop, and the five members elected by General Synod) are required between them to have special knowledge of architecture, archaeology, archives, art, history (including history of art and architecture), and liturgy (including church music). However, negotiations had ensured that membership was tipped towards those familiar with cathedral life, in particular worship and mission, rather than the standard heritage specialisms. Thus, of the 24 CFCE members (19 appointed by the Archbishops after consultation with various individuals or organisations, and five elected) the vice-chair and two deans must be selected in consultation with the representative body of deans; a bishop, in consultation with the House of Bishops; and two further members in consultation with the Chair of the Liturgical Commission. The five elected members must have knowledge of "cathedrals and the Church of England" and one must be a cathedral chapter member. In addition, a further two CFCE members must be or have been cathedral architects, and the Ecclesiastical Architects and Surveyors Association helps select a third architect or surveyor. Finally, one member is selected in consultation with the Director of the Royal School of Church Music. Thus more than half the members can be those associated closely with cathedral life, as clergy, congregation, or lay professional.

The remaining members bring relevant secular experience, and often deep specialist knowledge. The Chair, who must be a lay person, is appointed after consultation with the Secretary of State (currently the Secretary of State for Culture, Media and Sport), who also has a voice in the selection of one other member, as do each of the Chair of Historic England and the President of the Royal Academy of Art. The President of the Society of Antiquaries and the President of the Council for British Archaeology are both consulted about another member, and one architect or surveyor is selected in consultation with the President of the Institute of Civil Engineers. Finally, the Church of England advisory body, the Church Buildings Council, nominates three members of itself or of its specialist technical committees to the CFCE.

Perhaps surprisingly, these somewhat Gilbertian dramatis personae can be melded into a coherent and efficient determining body. In the event, the CFCE rarely votes, and when it does it is unlikely to split along factional lines. Rather, the accumulated knowledge of the realities of cathedral life, familiarity with the complexities of the physical fabric considerations, and the overriding purpose of the life sustained by the buildings provided by this membership are key contributors to a nuanced performance of the statutory role. At a smaller scale, at cathedral level, each FAC is composed of equal numbers proposed half and half by the cathedral chapter and the CFCE, to protect the independence necessary for the FAC to perform its statutory roles and the necessary close relationship to, and knowledge of, the individual cathedral. All members, at national CFCE and at cathedral FAC level, serve without payment.

However, while the cathedrals could with confidence look to bodies so constituted to be fully aware of their circumstances and aspirations, the long centuries of independence undoubtedly influenced the early years of the system's operation. Cathedrals took time to accommodate themselves to seeking approval for matters previously free from anyone else's concern and to appreciate the support the new system could offer if they chose to seek it. Undoubtedly, the additional cost and time commitments of the new system were irksome to some, and in consequence some aspects of the Measure, most notably each cathedral's obligation to have a Conservation Management Plan and an Inventory of historically significant items (each of which requires significant professional work), have still not been completed in some places. From its side, CFCE, with a small staff, was driven to focus in early years on implementing the basic mechanics required to operate the Measure, general guidance on statutory issues, processing applications, and its role in FAC membership.

By the second half of the 1990s, progress in implementing the spirit as well as the letter of the Measure was possibly helped by external events. The deans had recognized that recent problems in cathedrals which had caused public scandal were fundamental and must be addressed. The result was the creation of the Archbishops' Commission on Cathedrals chaired by Lady Howe which, in the 1994 report *Heritage and Renewal*, recommended many corporate governance, organizational, and management changes to bring greater consistency between cathedrals, and to provide accountability to wider interests. The Howe report endorsed the Care of Cathedrals Measure arrangements, and its own recommended organizational changes (enacted in the Cathedrals Measure of 1999) tended to increase the likelihood that cathedrals would have the human resources and capacity to take advantage of the existence of the CFCE, and hence helped to create favourable circumstances for better relationships.

INCREASED EXTERNAL FUNDING

A further impact was made by the Heritage Lottery Fund (HLF) and the sudden availability of its funding for large-scale projects, including provision of modern facilities to attract and retain visitors or to fulfil the enhanced educational role which the Howe Report had recommended to cathedrals. With the allure of possible multi-million-pound grants to supplement their traditional fundraising activities, cathedrals began to organize themselves to tackle large-scale projects and were more likely to seek early advice from the CFCE on projects and on handling the multiple constraints which might delay or prevent a worked-up application to the HLF. The opportunities for creative and supportive dialogue increased, and many cathedrals were better supported in identifying options for development works which could be successful. The CFCE and its staff built a broad institutional awareness of the range of problems and opportunities in different cathedrals which, taken together with the experience of individual members in their own professional spheres, particularly those working in the wider heritage environment, is now a significant resource. Its importance to cathedrals has increased as the availability of free advice from local planning authorities and Historic England has decreased under public expenditure constraints.

The CFCE has helped to identify and support funding for essential cathedral building works after the ending in 2009 of the scheme administered by English Heritage (see above). Between 2010 and 2013 the CFCE engineered and administered a scheme using Church of England funds and grants from the Wolfson Foundation and the Pilgrim Trust: this provided over £2.2 million for essential repair works. More recently, the existence of the CFCE system for determining cathedral works has underpinned the operation of the World War One Centenary Cathedrals Repair Fund, created and funded by HM Treasury in 2014, with further funding announced in 2015. The two rounds made £40 million available for essential works to the Church of England and Roman Catholic cathedrals in England. The CFCE secretariat designed the scheme, serviced an independent expert committee set up to recommend grants, and, under the auspices of the Archbishops' Council, administered the subsequent grant distributions.

CFCE engagement with cathedrals independent of specific projects is principally through the cathedrals section of the ChurchCare website (www.churchcare.co.uk) which provides, in addition to guidance through the legalities of scheme submission, policy guidance on aspects of project development which are common to most major schemes, ranging from considerations affecting access works in cathedrals, through lighting and sound installations, energy micro-generation, and the loan of objects, to the desirability of each cathedral creating a liturgical plan and an arts policy. This policy guidance is generally developed by member-level ad hoc or standing committees. CFCE also holds conferences on topical subjects, including stone policies, new art in cathedrals, and building environment monitoring, raising sponsorship to do so. It also maintains dialogue with FAC members through a triennial conference. For an individual project, the CFCE (on request) provides a delegation of members plus staff to discuss preliminary ideas on site, and as necessary repeats such visits, the delegation thus growing in its understanding and contribution as the project develops. Cathedrals are entitled to present their case in person to the full CFCE, and most large projects require more than one formal consideration to ensure all aspects are thoroughly covered and problems unravelled. The amount of time and the quality of advice and reflection devoted to each application can thus be significant, and generous in comparison with services available for free to owners of secular heritage buildings of high quality.

The system has operated robustly for twenty-five years, meeting the requirement for an accountable and defensible system of ecclesiastical exemption for cathedrals, and in the process also enhancing through both generic and specific advice the ability of cathedrals to develop good projects. It is for individual cathedrals to reflect on specific experience of the operation of this system. Not surprisingly, not every exchange results in a successful project, or a satisfied cathedral. Sometimes the heritage arguments prevail. Conversely, the heritage lobby has criticized some CFCE decisions permitting heritage loss, and some conservationists, principally the Victorian Society, have advocated that ecclesiastical exemption should be abolished and cathedrals (and churches) should be subject to all secular legislation. This has not so far been taken up as a cause by others, perhaps because the present system offers an accountable way of balancing the tension between heritage interests and those of the living church, and does so at significantly less cost than would a secular version of the system which operated to the same standard (were that possible within the limited conservation resources now available in local authorities). Both church and state are benefitting from the voluntary efforts of the CFCE members.

Over the CFCE's twenty-five years, the types of projects coming forward, and hence the issues faced, have expanded. Some cases still involve traditional topics: stone replacement programmes, conservation of stained glass windows and of objects, and minor archaeological investigations (fibre cable installation across closes causing many of the last). For these, the preferred starting point is the cathedral's Conservation Management Plan, if it exists, and—where appropriate—a professional method statement. A regular trickle of requests to loan outstanding items to other institutions continues, for which the CFCE has a standard checklist of conditions for consent to simplify the process. Other types of application seem to come in waves: for example, for glass doors to allow greater visibility into the cathedral and/or to improve draught control. Also traditional are free-standing re-ordering proposals, usually involving the making permanent of a previously temporary creation of a nave altar, with or without platform and associated liturgical furniture. For these, as for all internal changes, the CFCE now expects a cathedral to have developed a liturgical plan, which creates a context for the particular development. In 2011, the CFCE created a Liturgical Committee and published guidance to help cathedrals think through the impact on the building of current and possible future liturgical uses, reflecting theologically on worship practices, the congregational and other demands on the fabric, and the opportunities the building itself creates for new liturgical expression.

RETAINING A BALANCE

All the above types of applications can involve some heritage loss and the Commission needs to determine whether the benefits gained justify that loss. Should, for example, a cathedral be permitted, as part of a stone replacement programme, to replace worn stones at high level before they have completely eroded because they are temporarily accessible from scaffolding? Does the re-ordering of worship to a new location in the nave justify not only the provision of new, easily movable liturgical furniture but also the removal of an historic pulpit? It was to weigh up this sort of case that the CFCE was created.

However, other projects which now form a large part of the CFCE's work raise issues probably not in mind when the system was devised. The growth of cathedrals as tourist destinations during the second half of the twentieth century meant that the introduction of HLF funding in 1995, as noted above, has increasingly released a demand for larger, more complex projects. These frequently include the provision of substantial new structures for commercial facilities such as shops, catering outlets, and lettable space, or requirements to facilitate the use of the cathedral itself for non-worship purposes, such as moveable seating in place of pews, and additional lighting, heating, and sound systems to provide concert conditions. The CFCE recognizes that income generation is essential for the sustainability of cathedrals, and hence plays a role in forwarding the mission. But its powers do not extend to scrutiny of the financial case for any such proposals and it is a matter of chance whether anyone on the CFCE has significant experience of similar projects to guide them. In the absence of any other independent assessment of viability and sustainability, it is at the limits of prudent care for the heritage for CFCE to permit, without challenging the quality of financial and business analysis, irreversible heritage loss where the benefit is solely commercial.

Another implication of HLF grant applications is the requirement to make grant-aided facilities universally accessible (and, of course, cathedrals as part of their mission of welcome aspire more generally to meet modern secular standards of accessibility and to improve circulation). Inevitably, mediaeval buildings have many changes of level and often uneven flooring; some cathedrals wish to open triforia or tower spaces for new exhibitions, and others have crypts not safely accessible. In some places ramps are possible, and several examples have been successfully installed with little or no loss to the architectural or archaeological importance of the site. In others, accessibility can only be achieved by the installation of a lift.

The CFCE starting point for all these projects is that the cathedral needs to have developed a comprehensive access policy before bringing forward any proposals of this sort, and that, in addition to professional advice, both the cathedral architect and local people affected by disabilities should be enabled to take part in developing policy and plans. No member of the CFCE is selected to represent the interests of those who need enhanced access (its membership structure pre-dating the Disability Discrimination Act 1995), but the presence of practising architects ensures that the CFCE is aware of current best practice in this area. When a suitably supported application is made for a lift replacing an outmoded and often ugly version located between nave level and a raised chancel or choir aisle (often installed before the Measure came into force), CFCE considerations are usually confined to the appropriateness of the location for worship use and visitor circulation, the archaeological impact, and the design detail. Taller lifts, on the other hand, or ones which significantly intrude into the experience of a key cathedral space, have proved very problematic and there have so far been no successful applications for full-height lifts which are generally and detrimentally visible. HLF requirements for access can be satisfied by other than full access in such circumstances (e.g. access via audio-visual facilities) and cathedrals have been able to pursue their HLF applications successfully despite CFCE rejection of intrusive lift proposals. That the problem of tall lifts can be solved in some places is demonstrated both by the concealed lift which CFCE approved for the Winchester Bible exhibition project and by the lift and stair tower currently under construction at Westminster Abbey (which is not within CFCE jurisdiction), but a satisfactory design approach to location in the principal body of the cathedral has yet (if ever) to appear.

Another problematic application type which has increased in recent years is the permanent introduction of new art into cathedrals, a type which by its nature tends to be both high profile and contentious. A cathedral FAC is normally expected to handle applications concerning permanent additions to the fabric, but CFCE can call in any such application which it considers gives rise to special considerations. In addition, any work which constitutes a permanent alteration to the fabric is properly the concern of the CFCE, and many artworks satisfy this condition. Most significant new artworks are therefore submitted to the CFCE. These have included relatively conventional works, often in stone, sometimes replacing statues lost in historical times, and contemporary figurative or abstract works in many media, including digital. There is plentiful advice from such bodies as Art and Christian Enquiry about the best way to procure new art in ecclesiastical environments, although this is sometimes not followed by cathedrals. There is also a growing body of advice about maintenance and conservation considerations, particularly with new media work. The CFCE's own guidance is designed to help cathedrals provide an adequate context for the artist's brief, taking account of its relationship to other art in the cathedral, the theological intentions of the new commission, liturgical considerations, and the significance of the location. The primary concerns are the visual and physical impact of a proposed artwork on the existing heritage quality of its cathedral setting and any physical intervention in historic fabric. It is possible for the CFCE to have no reservations about the artwork per se, but to determine that its likely detrimental impact on the fabric or the context outweighs the benefits offered. The Commission is making the same judgement it makes in respect of any alteration or addition to the cathedral; that is, that the given and frequently complex historic artwork which is the entire cathedral should be protected and, if possible, enhanced unless the life of the cathedral requires otherwise. In the case of a new artwork, the distinction between this judgement and the exercise of taste is not always easy to explain and it is likely that it will continue to cause controversy.

Looking at progress since 1991, it is possible to see that many cathedrals have improved the quality of their custodianship of their buildings. Some of that improvement is directly attributable to changes in staffing levels at cathedrals, to greater and more sophisticated use of professional consultants, and to cathedrals raising their game in the competitive battle for public or lottery funds to do works. Some further improvement may in future owe something to the management training now available to deans which was introduced by Lord Green's 2014 report.[12] But some has probably resulted from the structured and co-operative approach adopted by the CFCE to its statutory role. Without the power to initiate schemes, it has sought to encourage the best proposals and to spread good practice.

CONCLUSION

There are still areas where innovative action by the CFCE could assist cathedrals to greater success. One is the work already underway to spread a better understanding of the importance of the science of the building environment before making proposals for new heating and ventilating installations, damp management, or conservation of objects. National conferences and dissemination of case studies are useful ways to introduce this topic to cathedrals, and to begin to address the insufficient understanding within the heating and services engineering profession and industry of the requirements of historic buildings in general, and large complex cathedrals with their atypical use patterns in particular. The CFCE also has a role to play in encouraging cathedrals to a better appreciation of the needs of their large and very important collections, whether of archives, manuscripts, plate, textiles, or other treasures. It is an area where a wider conversation needs to be had, and guidance issued, about the interaction between the disciplines of collection management, conservation, and display, tourism and exhibition practice, and the cathedral's life of worship and welcome. There is also scope for a national body such as CFCE to extend its search to identify and, if necessary, administer grants for cathedrals from sources which the cathedrals themselves cannot reach, and, in ways not available to the cathedrals acting together (as they increasingly do through the Association of English Cathedrals), to represent the cathedral perspective in discussion with government, Historic England, and the HLF. All these roles, alongside the existing activities, bring valuable professional resources to bear on problems which might escape attention, all at no direct cost to an individual cathedral, and at low administrative cost to the Church of England.

The system described above would not have been invented without the conflicting aspects of its historic origins, but it provides a continuingly effective way of marrying the interests of the modern church and the secular state in the survival and enhancement of these "most glorious national monuments". Credit for its success goes first to the individual members of the CFCE and of FACs, who have so generously given time and skills, and who carry out the statutory roles meticulously. Credit must also be paid to deans and chapters who have accommodated themselves to the legitimate interests of the wider world in these buildings. While the CFCE is, in the historical scheme, a recent addition to the cathedrals' world, it has, I suggest, earned its keep for the last twenty-five years and can continue to do so.

NOTES

1. Christopher Haigh, "Why Do We Have Cathedrals? A Historian's View", St George's Lectures No. 4 1998 (<https://www.perthcathedral.org/images/stories/LectureSeries_no4.pdf>), p. 11.

2. Lord Curzon of Kedleston, House of Lords Debate, 24 April 1913, *Hansard* Vol. 14 cols. 308–9.

3. Earl Beauchamp (First Commissioner of Works), "I am convinced that the introduction of ecclesiastical monuments into this Bill would create a host of difficulties which would make it far more difficult for the Bill to become law during the present session." House of Lords Debate, 24 April 1913, *Hansard* Vol. 14 col. 295.

4. Lord Kennet, " . . . there has recently been some discussion, both among the deans and within the Cathedrals Advisory Committee, of relationships between the Cathedrals Advisory Committee on the one hand and deans and chapters on the other hand. It would be true to say that neither side has been entirely content with the present procedure." House of Lords Question on Preservation of Cathedrals, 25 April 1967, *Hansard* Vol. 282 col. 522.

5. Church of England, *The Continuing Care of Churches and Cathedrals: Report of the Faculty Jurisdiction Commission* (CIO Publishing, 1984), para. 343, 123.

6. Church of England, *Heritage and Renewal: Report of the Archbishops' Commission on Cathedrals* (Church House Publishing, 1994), 199.

7. Lord Jellicoe, House of Lords Question on Preservation of Cathedrals, 25 April 1967, *Hansard* Vol. 282, col. 510.

8. General Synod (GS316A), *Agreement on State Aid for Churches in Use* (February 1976), Article (ix), quoted in *The Continuing Care of Churches and Cathedrals*, para. 2.

9. *The Continuing Care of Churches and Cathedrals*, para. 345, 124.

10. Section 1, The Care of Cathedrals Measure 2011.

11. The statutory amenity societies and Historic England are entitled to comment on all applications, and those relating to the exterior of the cathedral and its precincts are subject to normal local authority controls and listed building consent.

12. Lord Green Steering Group, *Talent Management for Future Leaders and Leadership Development for Bishops and Deans: A New Approach* (2014), available on the Church of England website (<https://www.churchofengland.org/media/2130591/report.pdf>).

4. HISTORY, HERITAGE, AND TAKING TIME

David Hoyle

CATHEDRAL HISTORIES

In November 1660, there was work to do at Durham Cathedral:

> The Deane and Chapter ... did unanimously resolve as
> a fruit of their Thankfullnesse to God to Resettle this
> Cathedrall upon the Antient Bottome of her Statutes and
> laudable customes ... [1]

In truth, their "Thankfullnesse to God" was probably qualified. The Dean
and four of the six prebendaries who met to make this resolution had just
returned from exile. Driven out during Cromwell's Commonwealth, there
were things they really could celebrate: a homecoming, the restoration
of the monarchy, and the return of both Anglican worship and cathedral
chapters (which had been abolished, by Parliament, in 1649). Their
problem was the cathedral itself. For three years, from 1650, it had served
as a prison for 3,000 Scots captured at Dunbar and now it was, they said,
"exceeding ruinous". [2] Dean and chapter were picking up the broken
pieces of their common life. If ever there was anything close to a fresh
start in the long history of Durham, this was it, and so we must notice the
backward glance. Dean Barwick and his colleagues, reeling from that tide

of innovation, knew where safety lay and settled themselves, comfortably, on that "Antient Bottome".

There is a common assumption that all of us who govern cathedrals, worship in cathedrals, or visit them, are still hard-wired to think as they did in Durham in 1660, and look backwards. If I tell people what I do, they occasionally smile and murmur the word "Barchester" (even though it is a fictional past they have in mind). I can live with that. Christianity makes a radical claim about what we encountered in the past; history is a fundamental part of our identity. It is really important, however, to ensure that it is only ever *part* of our identity.

In 2013, the Church of England website applauded the success cathedrals and churches enjoy in attracting visitors. It was kindly meant, but there was more than a suggestion that we are a superior kind of museum:

> They tell stories of kings, battles and wars, of brave men
> and women and of everyday life. These church buildings
> also contain a vast array of treasures from mediaeval wall
> paintings to original copies of the Magna Carta to beautifully
> crafted monuments and stained glass windows.[3]

That is what we think cathedrals should do, they should tell *stories*. There are lines from Sir Walter Scott on Prebends Bridge in Durham; you can fit them neatly into the frame of an iconic photograph of the cathedral:

> Grey towers of Durham
> Yet well I love thy mixed and massive piles
> Half church of God, half castle 'gainst the Scot
> And long to roam those venerable aisles
> With records stored of deeds long since forgot.[4]

The idea here is that what a visitor should come looking for, in Durham, is *history*. In a deliberately equivocal tribute to the achievement of Anglicanism, Simon Jenkins wrote:

> Cathedrals present themselves, like castles, as the
> great memorials to the nation's past. The two dozen

pre-Reformation survivors are, to me, the most beautiful things the English ever created. They are museums of mediaeval architecture, art, sculpture, stained glass and woodwork beyond compare.[5]

I am a historian, I like history, but I have to say, it is a qualified kind of "Thankfulnesse" you feel when you are admired because your history is what defines you. Cathedrals are becoming insects trapped in amber. Instead of being recognized for what we are, living communities with a past, there is an invitation to collude with an aesthetic that wants to make us historical exhibits. Glance backwards too often and what you get is a pain in the neck.

The all too easy association of history and cathedrals, the familiar assumption that we have "a story to tell", invites us to misunderstand our cathedrals. It also tempts us into some very bad history. When heritage becomes something you "manage", when it offers opportunities to volunteer, and when it is presented in such a way that it meets the "needs and interests" of visitors, we are in danger of doing something rather odd to history. Little by little we set boundaries around our history and turn it into something that exists in isolation from us. We begin to assume that it needs our help.[6] More positively, all the interest in the past has prompted some fine research and writing; we have never been better served with good historical writing about cathedrals.[7] It is a good moment to review our understanding of history and heritage and to ask some basic questions about our enthusiasm for telling a good story.

By the time that resolution was made at Durham, the statutes they described as "antient" were, in fact, a little over a hundred years old. They had been written, in some haste, in the furnace of the Reformation.[8] The "customes" they mentioned, however, could be traced back to a religious settlement that existed well before the Norman Conquest and to a cathedral priory created soon after it. Other cathedrals, Canterbury, Rochester, and London, were a thousand years old by 1660. At the beginning of the seventh century, when those three cathedrals were first built, they were not conceived as the things of beauty that Simon Jenkins goes looking for now. These were missionary centres assembled out of recycled material in the ruins of a civilization in retreat. They might have been small, but they were solid and deliberate echoes of a Roman past and a Roman culture. Built just a little later, Bishop Wilfrid's cathedral at York and his church at Ripon (which would much later become a cathedral) were more self-consciously imposing, "with walls of remarkable height and length". These two buildings, Jon Cannon tells us, "must have been mind-blowing".[9] In York and Ripon we can see the beginnings of a step change that would lead to the muscular mountains of stone that were built in the eleventh century, dwarfing the wooden homes that surrounded them. Thus, in a very short space of time, cathedrals were re-imagined, and we should notice that what is familiar to us now is not where the story began. The adjectives here are important: we are used to hearing that cathedrals are "beautiful", or "peaceful", but we must never forget that once they were defiant, radical, and unsettling.

Awkward and imposing partners in the urban landscape, these cathedrals could also be awkward places to live. The Norman invaders were a touch perplexed to discover that some of England's cathedrals were also monasteries. In Worcester, the bishop, Wulfstan, was also a monk, and generally reckoned to be a saint (he was finally canonized in 1203). Here was a cathedral that was a cultural and spiritual powerhouse.[10] In Canterbury, meanwhile, a Benedictine house was attached to the cathedral, but the community was an odd and uneasy amalgam of monastic and secular. The Archbishop, Stigand, was neither monk nor saint; indeed he was demonstrably corrupt, and arguably "the most secular of all archbishops" (despite the fact that there are a number of strong contenders for that accolade).[11] In Durham, the Normans met a community of married clergy in the cathedral that clearly had them baffled and at Rochester, a tiny college of canons were hanging on by their fingertips in a near ruin.[12] Meanwhile, in Ely, the church that would become a cathedral (in 1109) had been a stronghold for opposition to the Norman invasion. By contrast, in London, a bishop who had been appointed in 1051 welcomed the new king and was popularly known as William *the Norman*.[13] This was a chaotic patchwork of practice and politics that defied the Norman fixation for order and system. Across the country, the Normans encountered a variety of practice, a calendar of saints, and a range of devotion that was bewildering and unfamiliar. It was not one history, but several. Intriguingly, the new order accommodated the old. Not only did monastic cathedrals

survive, new ones were created. The story became more complicated still
when old foundations (at Selsey and Elmham) were abandoned to create
new cathedrals in both Chichester and, after some apparent indecision,
Norwich. Elsewhere, a commitment to staying in the same place could,
bizarrely, be anything but a vote for continuity. In Canterbury in 1070,
the new Norman archbishop, Lanfranc, swept away the old in favour of
a startling new creation that did not even pay lip-service to what had
been there before:

> ... a rejection of the previous building so complete that
> even its foundations were useless[14]

In York, similarly, the Normans made such a clean sweep that the site of
the older building remains uncertain.[15] The story of English cathedrals
is not linear. Bishops, and even deans and chapters, were not at ease with
their own heritage; they knocked down, re-imagined and rebuilt.

It takes a trained eye to remind us that we are heirs of a staggering
restlessness. At the end of the twelfth century something "febrile" was
afoot, with work at Canterbury, Wells, Lincoln, and York. In the 1220s
there was another great surge of building, a little more measured this time
perhaps: the west front at Wells, Salisbury, the south transept at York, the
rebuilding at Lincoln and Lichfield had things to say about episcopacy,
creating a church fit for great bishops.[16] Then in the early decades of
the fourteenth century there was new creation and a new intensity of
construction, at Exeter, the east end at Wells, the Lady Chapel at Ely. In
what has been called "the most artistically brilliant decade in English
architectural history", old assumptions were renewed with a changing
understanding of the demands of the liturgy and the devotions due to the
saints.[17] In this sense, cathedrals were shaped by a creative restlessness
that took different form in different places. Yet alongside all this new
brilliance there was often a deep social conservatism. You need to look
elsewhere for evidence of the major religious changes associated with the
arrival of the Franciscans and Dominicans, and our cathedrals were so out
of sorts with the victims of social injustice that, in the 1340s, they began
to turn themselves into fortresses, complete with defensive gatehouses.[18]

REVOLUTIONS IN HISTORY?

We forget, or ignore, the fact that the staggering achievements of mediaeval builders were fuelled by fresh ideas and a startling disregard for what they had inherited. Because cathedrals are such extraordinary survivors we look for continuities and, of course, we can find them. So, most strikingly of all, when reformation came it sometimes appears that it came gently. The shattered ruins at Rievaulx or Glastonbury are a glimpse of what might have happened at Rochester, or Durham, or Worcester. Instead, at Durham the last prior of the monastic community simply became the first dean. Indeed,

> The establishment of the new Chapter was carried through
> with as little disruption as possible, either to the estates of
> the priory or to the personnel of the community, over half
> of whom found posts in the new cathedral.[19]

At Durham they went on using the old paschal candle and a mediaeval image of Christ into the reign of Edward VI.[20] At Ely, it was the same story, as the prior, Robert Steward, meekly surrendered his monastery to the commissioners and was promptly rewarded with the Deanery.[21] At Canterbury, the shameless Prior Goldwell begged for the same favour, but he had long since exhausted everyone's patience.[22] Thus Nicholas Wotton was appointed dean, in 1541, but the newcomer was hardly marked by Protestant fervour and again, half the Catholic community made a smooth transition into a reformed church where candles burned and masses were said.[23] Small wonder that Collinson suggests that,

> only by a kind of legal fiction and under duress was
> Canterbury now a Protestant cathedral.[24]

Five monasteries that had been dissolved and faced ruin were rescued and turned into new cathedrals: at Bristol, Chester, Gloucester, Peterborough, and in Oxford (where a priory went through two changes of identity before emerging as the unique cathedral and collegiate foundation at Christ

Church). Westminster too was given a bishop, but that was a short-lived experiment. The old order was still plain to see.

This appearance of continuity, however, flatters to deceive. The first Protestant bishop of the new and reformed diocese of Bristol was an Augustinian canon, Paul Bush. On the face of it, this was another conservative appointment, harking back to Bristol's Augustinian past. Bush, however, embraced change, married, and had to be deprived of his preferment when Mary succeeded. He is now buried in the eastern lady chapel and his cadaver tomb, head resting on his mitre, makes a stark contrast with the surrounding abbots reclining in confident and vested pomp. In truth, Reformation was radical and whilst change might have crept up slowly, when it came it could be brutal and destructive. Thomas Cranmer himself was quite clear that he wanted to be rid of his own cathedral. In 1539 he had written:

> [F]or having experience both in times past and also in our days, how the said sect of prebendaries have not only spent their time in much idleness, and their substance in superfluous belly cheer, I think it not to be a convenient state or degree to be maintained and established.[25]

Reformation in Ely prompted the Bishop to insist that references to the Pope or to Becket were erased from every book. The great shrine of Etheldreda was destroyed in 1539 (Becket had gone from Canterbury in 1538 and Richard had been driven out of Chichester). Two years later, one hundred and forty-seven statues in the Lady Chapel were beheaded, in a staggering piece of sustained violence.[26] At St Paul's, there was radical preaching in the shadow of the cathedral and in 1538 the image of Our Lady of Grace was removed, as were a statue of St Uncumber and the Rood of the North Door. In Worcester, the great cult statue of Our Lady was taken down in 1537 and the tomb shrines of Wulfstan and Dunstan went five years later.[27] Reformation was not gentle at all; it arrived with axes and hammers. At Gloucester, a mediaeval reredos ablaze with saints was left shattered.[28] Everywhere, silver and vestments were sold and chantries ceased to function, the dead were abandoned, and the living were shut out of the communities they had loved so long and so well. Nor was reform done yet. When the Marian Catholic revival exiles returned, some of them had the light of battle in their eyes. In 1563 Durham got a new dean, a more radical figure, who swept away holy water stoups, burnt the banner of St Cuthbert, and defaced the tombs of mediaeval priors.[29] In St Paul's, Alexander Nowell campaigned against the use of the surplice, and in Oxford Thomas Sampson made a bonfire of popish vanities.[30]

Still there were those who longed for more. In 1572, John Field spoke for all the frustrated reformers:

> We should be too long to tell your honours of cathedral churches: the dens aforesaid of all loitering lubbers, where master Dean, master Vicedean, master Canons or Prebendaries the greater, master petty Canons or Canons the lesser, master Chancellor of the church, master Treasurer (otherwise called Judas the pursebearer), the chief chanter, singing men (special favours of religion), squeaking choristers, organ players, gospellers, pistlers, pensioners, readers, vergers, etc., live in great idleness, and have their abiding. If you would know whence all these came, we can easily answer you, that they came from the pope, as out of the Trojan horse's belly, to the destruction of God's kingdom. The church of God never knew them; neither doth any reformed church in the world know them.[31]

THE SEVENTEENTH CENTURY

The radicals finally got their chance when civil war broke out. Early in 1643 Parliament seized the assets of some deans and chapters, and soon afterwards pursued individuals known to be loyal to the king. Parliament had set its face towards Sion and knew that there would be no cathedrals there. Even so, it was not until the end of the war, in April 1649, that an ordinance finally abolished deans and chapters, and sequestrators began the work of asset stripping.[32] In Durham, as we have already observed, the cathedral was reduced to the role of prison. St Paul's became a barracks and even a stables. One appalled commentator thought that the animals were the least concern, as the cathedral had become

> a jakes for the worser beasts their masters, whose religion
> is Rebellion, whose piety is to blaspheme God [and] Revile
> ... the King ... [33]

In 1651 Great Yarmouth applied to buy Norwich Cathedral to use as a stone quarry.[34] Gloucester was, briefly, shot at in a siege and then became a preaching box; it took an energetic town clerk to prevent the city fathers from pulling it down.[35] Ely was so neglected that John Gauden, when he saw it shortly before the Restoration, called it "horribly desolate and ruined".[36] The life and worship of English cathedrals was changed beyond recognition. In Canterbury, a former soap boiler, turned Independent preacher, delivered sermons to a little company of saints in the Chapter House:

> We are as far away from the intention of a cathedral as it
> is possible to travel.[37]

All of which helps to explain why there might have been some constraints around the "Thankfullnesse" of the Durham Chapter in 1660. More significantly, it is a demonstration, if one were needed, that the "story" of English cathedrals is erratic, sometimes violent, full of radical reinvention, local, and peculiar. This is a history that confounds the idea that it could ever be something quite so straightforward as a "story". Christopher Haigh, in a sparkling essay about why cathedrals survived the Reformation, made just this point, celebrating the sheer rough and tumble of it all:

> I like my history messy, without the false neatness that
> rationalizing historians so often impose. I love cathedrals
> and choirs and Thomas Tallis and Herbert Howells and
> the Prayer Book and dignified worship and liberal-minded
> sermons. It's all terrific. But it was an accident.[38]

He went on:

> [H]istory is untidy and irrational—because it isn't purposely
> made by kings and politicians, it isn't planned by theologians
> and implemented by bishops. History is made by everyone,
> by people like us, who didn't know where they were going
> and hadn't got a big plan.

Haigh argues, here and elsewhere, that there was no such thing as "The
Reformation"; better, he says, to speak instead of "reformations". There
was no all-encompassing, managed process that made England Protestant;
rather there was a series of events, reforms, and setbacks to reform. As
he puts it in his lecture, "things just kept happening."[39] Other historians
of the Reformation, not least Eamon Duffy, might beg to differ and see
something more systematic at work. What Haigh highlights, however,
is the crucial point that the narrative is always more haphazard than we
usually pretend. English cathedrals do not offer us a history of continuity,
or a "heritage", or even "an inheritance of faith". What they have instead
is a glorious and muddled history in which there are indeed continuities,
but also times when a community resolutely turned its back on the
past, as well as occasional periods of literally shattering iconoclasm. In
Canterbury in 1643, Richard Culmer (known locally, and wonderfully, as
"Blue Dick of Thanet") climbed a forty-foot ladder to smash windows that
he considered idolatrous.[40] If we tidy this history up we just get it wrong.

HERITAGE OR HISTORY?

In 1994, the Report of the Archbishops' Commission on Cathedrals,
Heritage and Renewal, suggested that, for some at least, our buildings
articulate something that might otherwise not be said; they speak of "a
perception of the holy". So, the argument goes, there are those who can so
pick their way through stone, glass, and wood, and have an encounter with
something unfamiliar and transforming. For others, however, cathedrals,

conceived or adorned as great canopies over the bones of
saints, as stone reliquaries on an enormous scale, remain
still a witness to sanctity and an insight into fellowship
with past believers.[41]

That was the commissioners' rather elegant way of explaining that some
of us think that cathedrals are important for what they say now, whilst
some of us just hope they will say something about the past.

We are back at the conversation we might have with Simon Jenkins
about what cathedrals are for and why they matter. Setting aside, for the
time being, the worry as to whether or not cathedrals have become little
more than "museums", even a brief survey of just part of our history
begs the question why Jenkins, and so many others, seem to want to
stop the clock in the mediaeval past, where (they seem to think) a gentle
light falls through stained glass on the bones of the saints. There are two
problems here. Firstly, those bones are a fiction: they were scattered in
the 1530s and 1540s. Secondly, why is it that cathedrals are expected to
speak of *mediaeval* faith and practice? My own cathedral has a Norman
Chapter House, a thirteenth-century choir, and a Victorian nave. Who
decides that one trumps another? It is a particular kind of interest that
goes looking for flying buttresses instead of the music of Thomas Tallis,
or Charles Villiers Stanford, or the preaching of John Donne, or Henry
Parry Liddon. The determination to give us a "heritage", and name it, is
too often misleading and less than the truth.

There is, though, a more fundamental point about our history that needs
teasing out. The "messy" history we have inherited is a sharp reminder
of the sheer awkwardness of our engagement with the past. The story
is not just rich and complex, it takes twists and turns that can only be
explained by reference to politics, to social, to personal prejudices, financial
opportunity or constraint, and more beside. You have to work at it and
even then the "story" can elude you. As Rowan Williams has explained:

> The sense of the alienness and difficulty of the past should
> reinforce for the believer the sense of astonishment at the
> range of human expression and experience that can be
> counted as Christian.[42]

The point Williams makes is that, by engaging with our stubborn and clumsy past, we should learn some humility. It is not just that the story is not linear, is hard to tell, and full of contradictions. Inheriting this story, we have to acknowledge that we inherit the identity it confers. This is not a "story" we can tell as if we were describing a dusty artefact that can be safely returned to the neatly labelled box from which it came. This is *our* story; it had hold of us long before we got interested. We need to admit that we have been formed by what we have learned:

> We recognise ourselves and our concerns in a "distant mirror" . . . and so are reminded that we are not our own authors, that we have not just discovered what it is to be human, let alone what it is to be Christian.[43]

So it is not just that we are mistaken when we try to tidy our heritage up, making it simple when it is nothing of the sort. More seriously, the very exercise of going looking for our heritage demands a kind of arrogance that puts us in charge of a process that we never could control. History is supposed to remind us that it is we that have been shaped and formed. We simply cannot go to the library, or walk round a building, or listen to a guide and look thoughtful for a few moments, confident that we will then emerge clutching a thing called "heritage". History is the constant business of listening, looking, and adapting. Williams borrows from Brooke Foss Westcott, suggesting that what is asked of us is *labour*.[44]

In Bristol, a huge window in the north transept contains only a limited amount of stained glass. If you spend some time there you will eventually, perhaps, pick out the story of the Good Samaritan in small, busy panels of red and green. Underneath is a text, "Go, and do thou likewise." More than once I have heard visitors to the cathedral speak of this window fondly, seeing it as a prompt to social justice. They are right; that is indeed what the window intends. It *is* social commentary. It is also a challenge. In the first place, it was remodelled after bomb damage so it is yet another example of the messiness of what we inherit. More significantly, that text "Go, and do thou likewise" was the motto of one of Bristol's greatest benefactors, Edward Colston, who died in 1721. A text at the base of the window celebrates his name. It does that because his generosity provided education for the young and maintenance for the old from which the city still derives benefit. The trouble is that this was a liberality that owed some of its wealth to the traffic in slaves. Colston was deputy governor of the Royal African Company which, by the1680s, was transporting 5,000 slaves a year. Light from that window falls on the floor of the transept beneath and on memorials engraved with the words, "Of the West Indies": memorials, that is, to families who bought and sold slaves. The window, the memorials, the services at which Colston's name occasionally surfaces (when a school that still bears his name is present) cannot be described as part of our "heritage". They are, instead, the subject of vigorous contemporary debate around what we remember, how we remember, and the extent to which the present can judge the past. That is merely one aspect of the "labour" Williams describes.

It is a labour that demands humility from us all. Deans and chapters must be interrogated by the partners who help us understand and maintain our buildings and the artistic achievement within them. We must face, too, the challenge laid down by the Heritage Lottery Fund to think hard about the way the stories we tell can be heard by communities and visitors whose outlook might be different from our own. Sadly, the very strategies that are designed to help us do just that can sometimes serve to make us feel expert and impatient. As cathedral chapters work more assiduously at strategic planning they acquire paper plans that too quickly turn into promises we think we have made. Having done the planning we can come to resent a different point of view. The job of engaging with our history is corporate, communal, and that too is part of the *labour* that is required. There is a new depth and complexity to conversations we have with partners in local planning, Heritage Lottery Fund, and the Cathedrals Fabric Commission for England. There is a humility that deans and chapters have to learn and go on learning.

That said, those who write about cathedrals, and those who advise and challenge cathedrals, also need to commit to the long labour that interpretation and understanding requires. We are well served by men and women of deep learning and great generosity of spirit, but they too have to free themselves from too sharp a sense of what heritage might be and watch the terrible tendency to call "time", as if history might stop. Our cathedrals have never before been policed by communities so wary of change and so quick to deny that these are places that must be re-imagined and re-invented by new generations and new ideas.

CATHEDRAL DEVELOPMENTS

It is a commonplace to say that our cathedrals are probably in better repair than at any time in our history. We are fortunate indeed that there has been funding and expertise to tackle great projects, and fortunate in all the help we have received. There is a new ambition abroad. It is impossible not to notice that, when deans talk about the work of cathedrals, they talk about what they will do, what they might become. So, for example, James Atwell (who retired as Dean of Winchester in 2016) suggested that the distinctiveness of cathedrals lies in the way they look forward:

> Potentially they are alternative ways of expressing the life of the Community of Faith which for that very reason can offer inspiration to a Church often experimenting and casting around for new directions.[45]

Adrian Dorber (Dean of Lichfield), meanwhile, sees cathedrals as places of "huge creativity".[46] A research project he shared in commissioning was to help equip them for the job in hand, "to understand better the function they fulfil in society . . . "[47] The project's report sees them with a present task as places that convey "a sense of the spiritual and sacred."[48] Our partners know this, but they tend to start somewhere else. The Cathedrals Fabric Commission for England website (at the time of writing) does indeed talk about the fact that "cathedrals remain in use for their original purpose." It also says:

> The Church's cathedrals in England make an immense contribution to the country's historic environment.[49]

Similarly, the National Churches Trust website looks back more than it looks forward:

> [T]hose who venture inside are invariably rewarded and often surprised by what they find—bringing heart and depth to their destination experience. At a deeper level, churches and other places of worship are integral to the story of the places and communities within which they have evolved. They are signposts of our heritage, points where you can touch history, as well as places of visual and spiritual wonder.[50]

Together with partners like these and the Heritage Lottery Fund we need to forge a commitment to engage with the messiness of our own history and take care that careful process does not make us tidier than we should be.

Twenty-five years ago I bought a book about the "history debate". It was another of those moments when there was a row over what a history curriculum should look like; another argument about history needing a purpose and a clear narrative. One of the essays was by William Lamont, a distinguished historian of Puritanism. I did not know that he was once a school teacher. He described an agonizing attempt to teach eleven-year-olds about the Anglo-Saxon Witan. In the middle of his explanation a pupil put up his hand and asked, "Please sir, did the Anglo-Saxons wear gloves?" Later, he marked their essays:

> Hardly any had grasped the true nature of the Witan. On the other hand, every one of them began his essay: "The Anglo-Saxons were a group of people who did not wear gloves."[51]

His essay is a plea that we take our time. History is not understood easily, quickly. We come with the wrong questions, we rush off too quickly clutching the wrong prizes. He admires that "underrated educationist Mae West" who sang out her enthusiasm for "A Guy What Takes His Time".[52] That is the history we need; it really is all about taking time.

NOTES

1. Stanford Lehmberg, *English Cathedrals: A History* (Hambledon and London, 2005), p. 213.

2. Anne Orde, "From the Restoration to the Founding of the University 1660–1832", in David Brown (ed.), *Durham Cathedral: History, Fabric and Culture* (Yale University Press, 2015).

3. Janet Gough, Director of Church and Cathedral Buildings for the Church of England, quoted on the Church of England website at <https://www.churchofengland.org/media-centre/news/2013/03/thousands-visit-historic-churches-and-cathedrals.aspx>.

4. Lines from Walter Scott, "Harold the Dauntless", carved on Prebends Bridge; J. R. Watson, "The Cathedral in Literature", in Brown, *Durham Cathedral*, p. 484.

5. Simon Jenkins, "There is one sure way to save our ailing churches", *The Guardian*, 10 October 2016.

6. See the Heritage Lottery Fund website, <https://www.hlf.org.uk/looking-funding/difference-we-want-your-project-make>.

7. See, for example, Brown, *Durham Cathedral*; Jon Cannon, *Cathedral: The Great English Cathedrals and the World That Made Them, 600–1540* (Constable, 2007); Patrick Collinson, Nigel Ramsay, and Margaret Sparks (eds.), *A History of Canterbury Cathedral* (Oxford University Press, 1995); Derek Keene, Arthur Burns, and Andrew Saint (eds.), *St Paul's: The Cathedral Church of London 604–2004* (Yale University Press, 2004); Peter Meadows and Nigel Ramsay (eds.), *A History of Ely Cathedral* (Boydell Press, 2003).

8. Durham does not have a surviving set of Henrician statutes, and we do not know if they ever existed; new statutes were provided in the reign of Queen Mary I. I am grateful to the archivists at Durham for help on this point.

9. Cannon, *Cathedral*, p. 41; I am deeply grateful for Jon Cannon's guidance in commenting on a draft of this essay.

10. Frank Barlow, *The Feudal Kingdom of England, 1042–1216*, 2nd edition (Longmans, 1961), p. 37.

11. Nicholas Brooks, "The Anglo-Saxon Cathedral Community, 597–1050" in Collinson et al., *A History of Canterbury Cathedral*, p. 33.

12. David Rollason, "The Anglo-Norman Priory and its Predecessor 995–1189" in Brown, *Durham Cathedral*; Lionel Butler and Chris Given-Wilson, *Medieval Monasteries of Great Britain* (Michael Joseph, 1979), p. 327.

13. Keen, "Ely Priory" in Meadows and Ramsay, *A History of Ely Cathedral,* pp. 41ff; Pamela Taylor, "Foundation and Endowment: St Paul's and the English Kingdoms, 604–1087" in Keene et al., *St Paul's,* pp. 15–16.

14. Cannon, *Cathedral,* p. 69.

15. Ibid., p. 463.

16. Ibid., pp. 99–105.

17. Ibid., pp. 124–126.

18. Robert Grosseteste was an exception; Cannon, *Cathedral,* pp. 109, 118.

19. William Sheils, "From Reformation to Restoration, 1539–1660" in Brown, *Durham Cathedral,* p. 81.

20. Ibid., p. 82.

21. Ian Atherton, "The Dean and Chapter, 1541–1660" in Meadows and Ramsay, *A History of Ely Cathedral,* p. 170.

22. Patrick Collinson, "The Protestant Cathedral 1540–1660" in Collinson et al, *A History of Canterbury Cathedral,* pp. 151–152.

23. Ibid., pp. 159–160.

24. Ibid., p. 162.

25. Henry Jenkyns (ed.), *The Remains of Thomas Cranmer* (Oxford University Press, 1833) Vol. 1, p. 292.

26. Atherton, "The Dean and Chapter", pp. 172–173; Collinson "The Protestant Cathedral", p. 154.

27. Diarmaid MacCulloch, "Worcester: A Cathedral City in The Reformation", in Patrick Collinson and John Craig (eds.), *The Reformation in English Towns 1500–1640* (Macmillan, 1998), pp. 100–101.

28. David Hoyle, "Reformation and Civil War" in Susan Hamilton et al., *Gloucester Cathedral: Faith, Art and Architecture: 1000 Years* (Scala Books, 2011), p. 55; there is some debate about the date of this iconoclasm.

29. Sheils, "From Reformation to Restoration", p. 85.

30. David J. Crankshaw, "Community, City and Nation, 1540–1714" in Keene et al., *St Paul's,* p. 51; Lehmberg, *English Cathedrals,* p. 161.

31. John Field, "A View of Popish Abuses", in H. C. Porter (ed.), *Puritanism in Tudor England* (Macmillan, 1970), p. 133.

32. Collinson, "The Protestant Cathedral", p. 199.

33. Crankshaw, "Community, City and Nation", p. 63.

34. Collinson, "The Protestant Cathedral", p. 201.

35. Hoyle, "Reformation and Civil War", pp. 63, 65.

36. Atherton, "The Dean and Chapter", p. 192.

37. Collinson, "The Protestant Cathedral", p. 202.

38. Christopher Haigh, "Why Do We Have Cathedrals? A Historian's View", St George's Lectures No. 4, 1998 (<https://www.perthcathedral.org/images/stories/LectureSeries_no4.pdf>), p. 13.

39. Ibid., p. 6.

40. Collinson, "The Protestant Cathedral", pp. 196–197.

41. Quoted in Lehmberg, *English Cathedrals*, p. 299.

42. Rowan Williams, *Why Study the Past? The Quest for the Historical Church* (Darton, Longman and Todd, 2005), p. 111.

43. Ibid.

44. Ibid, p. 112.

45. James Atwell, "Les grands projets", in Stephen Platten and Christopher Lewis (eds.), *Dreaming Spires? Cathedrals in a New Age*, (SPCK, 2006), p. 131.

46. *Spiritual Capital: The Present and Future of English Cathedrals* (Theos and The Grubb Institute, 2012), p. 9. Available to download from the Theos website (<http://www.theosthinktank.co.uk/publications/2012/10/12/spiritual-capital-the-present-and-future-of-english-cathedrals>).

47. *Spiritual Capital*, p. 10.

48. *Spiritual Capital*, p. 11.

49. See cathedrals section of ChurchCare website (<http://www.churchcare.co.uk/cathedrals/the-cathedrals>).

50. Andrew Duff of Inspired Northeast quoted on the National Churches Trust website (<http://www.nationalchurchestrust.org/know-your-building/understanding-places-worship>).

51. William Lamont, in Juliet Gardiner (ed.), *The History Debate* (Collins and Brown, 1990), p. 28.

52. Ibid., p. 34.

5.   CATHEDRAL-SHAPED WORSHIP

Stephen Platten

A CATHEDRAL SHAPE?

> The nature and architecture of church buildings and their
> context relate directly to the liturgy and what buildings
> say theologically.[1]

So runs the abstract of an article which looks at the relationship of church
buildings more generally to the liturgy. Cathedrals are a "sub-set" of
the wider species of church buildings, and similar implications apply.
So "cathedral-shaped" refers to the architecture of the buildings and its
relation to the liturgy but it refers to more than these, for the buildings
are nothing apart from the people or even *communities* who inhabit them.
Who makes up the liturgical community within a cathedral, or are there
many different communities? Remembering the multivariety of services,
worship styles and liturgies to which cathedrals are hosts, there is often a
preliminary question to answer—whose service is this anyway? Each of
these questions presupposes that there is some sort of strategy or broader
understanding of the nature of each individual cathedral building, in other
words, a flexible liturgical plan—how is the building to be understood in
relation to regular worship, special services, liturgies focused on the bishop,
the route of pilgrims through the cathedral building, and opportunities
for silent prayer and recollection? So cathedral-shaped worship describes
not one single consistent "performative liturgical act" but instead a range

of activities, all of which are ultimately and primarily about the *opus Dei*
for that is these buildings' raison d'être.

ORIGINS OF THE LITURGICAL COMMUNITY

We must begin somewhere, however, so perhaps the essential starting
point is the local or even resident liturgical community. Who does this
describe? Some historical reflection can set this in context. In the early
part of 1995, the house in the north-east corner of the Lower Close
Green in Norwich Cathedral Close was being refurbished in preparation
for its new occupants. One of the most alarming discoveries was of an
enormous unplaned horizontal beam, which was unsupported at its
eastern end, within the house itself. As measures were taken to secure the
beam, further research was carried out. The beam was neither planed nor
prepared nor finished, as it was simply the felled trunk of a tree which
had been used centuries before as a supporting beam in the Great Barn
of the cathedral priory. Further research revealed that this tree trunk ran
all the way through the range of houses on the north side of the Lower
Close Green, terminating within the house which stands on the eastern
side of the curtilage of the Deanery.

So this complete range of houses is simply a reworking of the structure
of the Great Barn, doubtless with myriad further changes in successive
centuries. Indeed, on the north side of one of the houses, the portal of
the doorway is nothing less than the apex of the Gothic arch of one of
the series of openings into the barn through which carts, animals, and
even ploughs might have entered. In later centuries, deposits of soil have
meant that the height from the ground to that apex has been significantly
reduced. We are told by dendrologists that this tree would almost certainly
have been growing as a sapling at the time of the eleventh century Norman
conquest of England. Our story is worth pursuing further since it opens up
to us the provenance of the earliest liturgical community in the cathedral.
On the east side of this same Close Green are houses on the footprint of
the old bakehouse and brewhouse—elements of these buildings remain.

The south-west corner of the close was occupied by the mediaeval church of St Mary-in-the-Marsh: at the time of writing this parish still exists and worships monthly in the cathedral,[2] even though the church was demolished as long ago as 1564. The very fine seven-sacrament font in St Luke's Chapel in the cathedral is the sole survivor of the church. So here is one other rather unusual liturgical community.

At the western end of this same green are the fragmentary remains of the infirmary. Some fifteen years ago, while refurbishing a building nearby, one building worker fell through some six feet into part of the remains of the old monastic drain which ran along the south side of the infirmary. The south-eastern entrance to the cloister is still known as the "Dark Entry". It was the final doorway through which a monk would pass on his way to the infirmary and thence on his journey back to his Creator and Redeemer.

THE MONASTIC PATTERN

The story that these buildings tells, then, is of the Benedictine priory which both ran the cathedral and was its resident "liturgical family". Its titular head, or abbot, was the bishop and its effective working head, the prior; Norwich was unusual in having a mitred prior alongside the mitred bishop. A similar tale to this could be told of all the cathedral churches of the "new foundation". So, to a greater or lesser extent, the buildings (often adapted, sometimes ruinous, and in certain cases no longer extant) can be traced around these former Benedictine priories, in Canterbury, Durham, Winchester, Worcester, Gloucester, Ely, Peterborough, Rochester, Chester, Bristol, and St Albans. Bristol, Gloucester, Chester, and Peterborough have been cathedrals only since the time of Henry VIII. St Albans has been a cathedral only since 1877. Carlisle too is a cathedral of the new foundation, having been an Augustinian priory before the Reformation. "New foundation" simply refers to Henry VIII giving the cathedrals new statutes when the monastic communities were dissolved.

The legacy of these earliest cathedral liturgical communities remains, albeit with discontinuities. The pulpitum screen marked the dividing line between the monks' church and the people's church. This is a reminder that, from the beginning, the liturgical community in the monastic cathedrals included an engagement with the wider world. In Norwich, this engagement was not always positive, and in the riots of 1272 the cloister was effectively razed to the ground.[3] There is ample evidence, however, of laity from the wider community coming to the cathedral. Margery Kempe, for example, recounts coming to "the Trinity" at Norwich in order to be shriven.[4] The hostry building would be where the Benedictine welcome to all "as if they were Christ"[5] would be made plain; the locutory between the hostry and the cathedral would be where the laity met their interlocutors to be shriven or for counsel. With the advent of the Reformation, so these cathedrals were re-founded with the Prior becoming the Dean.[6] The monastic liturgical community ceased to exist from then onwards.

We have focused here intentionally on the former Benedictine (and Augustinian) cathedrals since the origins of the liturgical community are very clear. The Church of England inherited significant elements of this Benedictine tradition; capacious vicarages and rectories continued to offer the possibility of hospitality and welcome. Durham, Norwich, and other Benedictine foundations continue to cherish their monastic roots, in certain cases reading from the Rule of St Benedict daily during the singing and saying of the offices and elsewhere leading study courses and residential gatherings which honour still the principles enshrined in the rule.[7]

OLD FOUNDATIONS AND NEWER CATHEDRALS

Cathedral churches of the "old foundation" also had their own nucleus of community in the continuity of the chapter and a company of prebends or prebendaries down the centuries. Here there was no need to re-found the cathedrals, which could continue effectively as before: there was continuity also, then, with the liturgical community rooted in the dean and prebends. Here the cloisters were effectively ceremonial walkways, without the same nodal significance as in the monastic foundations. The choral foundation continued and survives and prospers today. It remains a key part of the liturgical community which itself acts as the kernel of every cathedral's worshipping life.

The history of cathedrals since the Reformation has varied from place to place, and has, of course, included new foundations in the nineteenth and twentieth centuries, as the Church of England responded to changes in demography. The community relating to the mediaeval cathedrals has continued to change and develop, and especially where cathedrals are surrounded by a close or a precinct.[8] Often the liturgical community had been enriched by the contribution of those living within the precincts. Most cathedrals not only say or sing the daily office, morning and evening, but also celebrate a daily (often early morning) Eucharist. Alongside this small community stands the choral foundation which has continued to remain at the heart of all cathedrals. Indeed, where new cathedral foundations have been established, almost universally the establishment of a choral foundation alongside all else has been a key element in the new cathedral's life and at the heart of its worship.

We have alluded to the discontinuities effected by the Reformation, but perhaps most remarkable is the continued inheritance, an inheritance adapted where newer cathedrals now thrive. The unchanging rhythm of the daily office remains the heart's blood of English cathedrals, and the pattern of the monastic foundations underpins the contemporary life of these "collegiate" churches, marking them out from the majority of parish worship patterns. Some abbeys and great churches parallel cathedral culture, but only a handful—including Westminster Abbey and St George's Chapel, Windsor—have the resources to power a similar "kernel-like liturgical community" at the heart of the foundation. An interesting confluence of the Benedictine influences and Thomas Cranmer's desire for a pattern of daily worship has acted as the substrate or framework upon which the rest of a cathedral's life may hang. This pattern is an adaptation of what liturgical scholars describe as the "cathedral office" in contrast to the "monastic office". It fashions still the discipline and offering of daily prayer in the English cathedral tradition.[9]

DIVERSITY IN UNITY

Having established the existence of a liturgical community at the heart of
cathedral worship, it is also the case that the strength of this community,
and the discipline which it lives, acts as the essential structure allowing a
cathedral to remain hospitable to a wide diversity of different demands
and traditions. So cathedrals are sustained by this kernel-like community,
but this community neither owns the building nor all the worship that
happens within it. Other dynamics and other constituencies bring into
play a resonance which allows for tradition and innovation, continuity
and creativity, stability (a key element within Benedict's rule), and an
openness to a wider world. One of the first starting points in exploring
the variety implied here is the manifold number of stakeholders who
believe the cathedral is "their cathedral". The obvious starting point here
is the diocesan bishop, since there would be no cathedral in that place but
for the bishop and the bishop's chair, the focus for teaching, the *cathedra*.
It is frequently although not uniquely the case that the bishop ordains
deacons and priests within the cathedral. In that sense it is the nursery
of new clergy—the cathedral is midwife to the process. Increasingly,
bishops have come to focus the sacraments of initiation, that is, baptism-
confirmation, within their cathedral churches. The use of stational liturgies
for baptism and confirmation is both easier because of the greater space
available in most cathedrals, and also, when performed imaginatively, it
leaves a permanent mark on the minds and hearts of those being baptized
and confirmed. This is reinforced when the drama of worship, including
colour, light, music, and movement, is recognized and employed. The
focus of baptism and confirmation at the Paschal Vigil on Easter Eve
continues to increase across English cathedrals and recaptures the drama
of the pattern of preparation throughout Lent which led into the liturgical
cycle at Easter in the early Church, in what have been described as the
"awe-inspiring rites of initiation".[10]

Different imaginative patterns have developed with regard to the
Paschal Vigil. In Portsmouth (and later in Norwich and Wakefield), the
use of light at the vigil was for dramatic purposes: a gas "flame machine"
which was ignited as the "New Fire". As the Old Testament readings
were proclaimed, so the flame would burgeon and die back. When the

call from the Genesis reading was, "Let there be light", so duly the flame rose; similarly as the waters of the Red Sea were parted and as Jonah was spewed forth from the great fish. Each time, after these dramatic moments, the flame would die back. The impact of these vast darkened enclosures of transcendent space is potent indeed. Similar patterns continue to be developed elsewhere, and indeed outside the particular realm of cathedrals.

LITURGIES FOR THE CHURCH

The bishop, of course, is the focal representative of the local church, but alongside this there are other intra-Church stakeholders who vie for their part in cathedral life. The effect of the twentieth-century "ecumenical movement" has been to make the cathedrals of the Church of England the property of all Christian people within an area or region. Holy Week is often a good indication of this: both clergy and laity of the free churches will often find their way into cathedrals for the rich liturgical banquet which may be provided all the way through from Palm Sunday to Easter Day. Advent and Christmas, too, can offer similar opportunities. In one cathedral, the colleges and university came together to fabricate the set for a live crib which was set in the cloister and used in both crib services for children, and in procession for other Christmas services, whilst at the same time acting as a living tableau of the meaning of Christmas to visitors and pilgrims. Even the ducks and chickens were hatched from eggs and nurtured by students at the local agricultural college! Only the expanded space of the cloisters easily makes this possible, although smaller cathedrals in key city spaces might well consider establishing something similar.

Diocesan training agencies, and notably in liturgy, frequently use cathedrals, and the precentor often chairs or acts as consultant to diocesan liturgical committees and groups. Then, too, groups with "special interests" are keen to use these buildings which enclose such volumes of "transcendent space". So "prayer and praise" evenings, youth worship with rock bands, and charismatic gatherings test the flexibility and generosity of those of a more urbane and traditional liturgical culture. Musical organizations too, from the Royal School of Church Music, the Guild of Church Musicians, and the Royal College of Organists, all the way through to local sacred music societies are keen to avail themselves of the expertise and the unique space within these buildings.

STAKEHOLDER LITURGIES

All of these agencies and groups remain still fairly clearly within the bounds of the Church as an institution, albeit at differing levels of distance from "official church circles". But what of other stakeholders? Educational institutions are a prime example. Where there are ancient school foundations locally, cathedral naves have often become the venue for daily or weekly worship. The space and resources offer remarkable opportunities for the encouragement of imagination of students within a rich historical context. But increasingly cathedrals act also as key foci for local schools, both church-sponsored and maintained. The use of drama, pilgrimage, role play, and stational liturgies can take myriad different forms. Cathedrals cease to be merely galleries of art and culture, or the backdrop for historical study. They become places where the Christian faith is not merely described but rather becomes performative, as is the very nature of faith. For this to be successful, an element of risk is necessarily involved—the liturgy becomes not solely the property of the cathedral foundation; there is a symbiosis between the resident community and the pilgrims, visitors and members of the cathedral's wider community.

From beyond the bounds of this educational engagement with the liturgy enter the legions of other groups within a region who *know* the cathedral is theirs too. The Rotary Club wish to celebrate their centenary; the Lord Lieutenant decides to honour all who give in countless ways in the voluntary sector; the local regiment comes to lay up its colours; the high court judge comes to pray at the start of his session, or indeed asks for a fully blown "Justice Service" for the "great and the good" and all others involved in the police and judiciary; all the local clearing banks claim the cathedral for their own as they invite clients and staff alike to a Carol Service or Christmas Festival; the Freemasons (much thinner on the ground than in the past) ask if they can have a service—how should the cathedral foundation respond? The Scouts, Guides, Air Training Corps, Sea Cadets, and numerous other uniformed organizations all wish to come; the county agricultural society and the remnants of the National Union of Mineworkers come to remember and to give thanks, and so the list could be continued. What might the cathedral make possible?

Most cathedral deans, early on in their time (perhaps alongside residentiary canons), will have made their progress through the diocese to make clear their openness and enthusiasm for all to come, be it through a tour of the deaneries, or through individual visits. Often, when called to speak, they will catalogue perhaps a score of groups and organizations all of whom see themselves as stakeholders in the cathedral. Almost certainly their audience will be able to add at least half a dozen more to that list. This has also been the opportunity for deans and chapters to repeat invitations to individual parishes and deaneries to make pilgrimage to the cathedral, and perhaps to integrate these pilgrimages with the diocesan cycle of prayer. All this requires vast stamina by cathedral staff. It calls out of the clergy chapter and lay teams imagination, of the vergers stamina, of the administrators logistical juggling, and of the financial team a real care to make as many welcome as is humanly possible without unrealistic budgetary demands being placed upon them. The cathedral circus for the home-and-away stakeholders bears close similarities with the background to the fairground "big top", whilst at the same time never losing that essential core of worship and devotion which is the cathedral's raison d'être and lifeblood. So how does the building itself speak to all this? How does it go with the grain and how does it challenge even the most imaginative teams of liturgical professionals? How might liturgies for this great variety of stakeholders be imagined and performed?

BUILDINGS SHAPING LITURGY

If, as was hinted earlier in this book, it is often difficult for people to identify what might be their "favourite" cathedral, then one of the reasons for this is the sheer variety of different buildings, even within these shores. No two cathedral buildings are identical. Indeed, this variety can also be a cause for challenge or frustration in looking to liturgical creativity and imagination: "If only we had a longer nave; if only there were not that screen halfway down; if only the transepts were just that much bigger; if only there were more space in the choir", and other "if onlys" could be added. There are obvious limitations in different cathedrals. Many which were once parish churches have significantly less space than those (often built concurrently with larger parish churches) built as cathedral churches from the beginning. Conversely, the opposite can be an equal challenge: the naves of Lincoln, York, and Ely are vast, so real imagination is required to see how best to order them liturgically and to use them with an imagination which embraces a proper "human" scale. Carlisle is unique in being truncated by the loss of its nave after the siege during the Civil War in the mid-seventeenth century, and thus presents a different set of challenges.

CATHEDRALS AS SACRAMENTAL

Before we engage more fully, however, with the different patterns, shapes, and designs of cathedrals, it is worth pausing to reflect on their nature and raison d'être, and indeed that of all church buildings. How are they to be understood and developed? Some of these issues have been explored in our first chapter, but a kaleidoscope of almost accidental opportunities intrude positively. So, in one cathedral some years ago, a generous donor offered the money necessary to place a permanent sign of the passing of Christianity's second millennium. It was agreed to commission windows and a proper commissioning process was established. When the artist was finally chosen, the donor was surprised that the cathedral chapter had not simply put the commission out to competitive bidding: "That's what I did when I replaced my garage roof last year", he reflected. But cathedrals and church buildings are not purely functional in the same way as an official building, an industrial structure, or even domestic housing, however grandiose any of these might be. For there is something of a sacramental nature defining these buildings themselves.[11]

It would be a crude use of theological language to see the buildings as sacraments, in the classic sense, but their sacramental and liturgical purpose lends much to such a description. This is no new discovery. It was explored to some degree, for example, in William Golding's powerful novel, *The Spire*.[12] In the mind and heart of the dean, the cathedral became the dynamo or "demon" which powered his vision. A rediscovery of such sacramental language for churches and cathedrals began in the nineteenth century. Many of the outstanding exponents of the Gothic Revival, George Gilbert Scott, G. F. Bodley, William Butterfield, G. E. Street, and John Loughborough Pearson, were devout worshippers themselves. Indeed, Pearson is frequently quoted as saying that, as an architect, "My business is to create a building which will bring people soonest to their knees." Another celebrated Victorian designer, Charles Eamer Kempe, had actually sought ordination. Suffering from a severe speech impediment, however, he decided to channel his devotion into the artistry of stained glass design. Benjamin Webb and John Mason Neale translated William Durandus' *Rationale Divinorum Officiorum* into English, focusing particularly on sacramentality. Their translation runs:

> We assert, then, that *Sacramentality* is that characteristic which so strikingly distinguishes ancient ecclesiastical architecture from our own. By this word we mean to convey the idea that, by the outward and visible form, is signified something inward and spiritual . . . This Christian reality, we would call SACRAMENTALITY; investing that symbolical truthfulness, which it has in *every* true expression, with a greater force and holiness, both from the greater purity of truth which it embodies.[13]

It is not necessary to affirm every aspect of their sometimes polemical language in accepting the essential point about sacramentality. This notion has been explained in more detail elsewhere, but it is a crucial starting point for understanding the way in which cathedral buildings help shape the liturgy and vice versa.[14] It indicates something of the nature of the worship which takes place within church buildings, and in this case specifically cathedrals. At its most elemental this sort of language is being applied when the spires are said to point towards the heavens, thus identifying the purpose of church buildings. Such imagery does not automatically suggest belief in a God who is "an old man beyond the skies"; instead it suggests that churches themselves can be outward and visible signs of something more profound and transcendent. A similar piece of imagery was used of cathedrals in an earlier book, entitled simply *Flagships of the Spirit*; the towers of Norfolk churches, largely placed at the west end of these buildings, seemed to group around the spire of Norwich Cathedral, which figuratively appeared as the flagship of this fleet or flotilla of the spirit.[15]

SACRAMENTAL SHAPES

Moving to rather more precision, the ground plans and structure of cathedrals themselves speak of theology. For example, many early cathedrals and churches took up the Roman basilican pattern. The basilica was the main meeting hall within the forum of a Roman city. Here the local prefect, representing the Emperor, would have a public seat, not dissimilar in principle to the bishop's *cathedra*. He would be surrounded by his key advisors when there was a public gathering of an official nature. In some places, churches stand on the site of a former Roman basilica, perhaps responding to Pope Gregory the Great's advice to Augustine of Canterbury, not to destroy pagan temples but to transform them and ultimately "Christianize" them.[16] A supreme example of a Roman basilica is the surviving *Aula Palatina* in Trier in Germany. This, however, would have been a royal hall and not a place of worship. A perfect example of an early basilican *church* is St Sabina on the Aventine Hill in Rome. The basilica is classically a rectangular building with an apsidal end. In the imperial hall, the prefect would sit in the centre of the apse with his advisors on either side in a semi-circular arrangement. A cathedral basilica would adopt the same pattern with the bishop at the centre of the apse and his key supporting clergy surrounding him. This basilican conclusion to a cathedral is particularly prevalent in France, where the apsidal end was sometimes developed into a corona of smaller chapels.

This French pattern, however, moves us a stage further on, for frequently the western arm of the cathedral would include an extended nave, flanked by two (or sometimes four) transepts, north and south of the main axis. This produces in plan a cruciform structure. The building itself takes the form of a *cross*. We cannot know definitely whether this was a purely architectural development or whether it was a deliberate inclusion of the image of the cross. The classical pattern of that being described here in an English cathedral is Norwich. Herbert de Losinga was a Benedictine monk from Fécamp in Normandy who founded the new cathedral and moved it from Thetford to Norwich, deliberately opting for the French pattern, and almost as an intentional archaism. He saw himself as the lineal successor of the seventh-century Roman missionary to East Anglia, St Felix. Herbert even had an effigy of Felix placed over the door of the north transept next to his own palace, to remind people of the bishop's pedigree as they entered the cathedral from his residence.

This discussion, then, has moved us into the realm of cruciform buildings via the earlier basilican form. A further crucial development needs to be logged at this point. Cathedrals were frequently now becoming multi-room buildings, both through the proliferation of chapels and through screens frequently appearing at the crossing marking off the monks' church, or the chapter's church in secular cathedrals, from the people's church, the nave. Clearly each of these variations in cathedral architecture has an impact on possible liturgical patterns and ordering within the different buildings.

SHAPING THEOLOGY

These steps, and especially the identification of separate rooms within cathedral buildings, move us on one further stage. A number of English cathedral buildings have had their buildings radically affected by devotion to a saint and the building of a shrine. So, for example, Lincoln's east end originally terminated in an apse, but with the building of the shrine of St Hugh and the construction of the St Hugh's Choir, an extended rectilinear east end was constructed; in Lincoln, the pattern of two earlier east ends is traced out on the floor of the easternmost part of the building. In Durham and in St Albans, an elaborate shrine was built east of the high altar, both of which can still be appreciated.[17] Pilgrims continue to come to pray at these shrines. Both Chichester and Winchester have similar rectilinear east ends to house the shrines of their respective saints. Canterbury, alongside Durham the most popular of mediaeval cathedral pilgrimage destinations, is more interesting still. Following Becket's martyrdom in 1170, the shrine and place of pilgrimage was established first in the so-called "Martyrdom" in the north-west transept. Later, in 1220, the shrine was translated and rebuilt in the Trinity Chapel, in the far eastern arm of the cathedral. This allows a further theological reflection on the shape of the building now. On entering the nave, Henry Yevele's vast perpendicular space is a natural place to reflect on God's fatherhood as Creator. Standing at the top of the steps of the crossing, with the Martyrdom to the north and where the two main arms of the cathedral intersect, reminds one of Christ and the redemptive works of God. Moving finally into the Choir and on to the Trinity Chapel one is cocooned in the space of the Spirit and the saints. It is a powerful image of the Trinity, where God in Trinity fills the entire cathedral space and where it is impossible to separate different parts of the cathedral from each other. In the same way, God in Trinity cannot dissolve into tritheism or allow any of the hypostases of God to stand alone.

This swift tour of a limited number of English cathedrals has demonstrated two essential elements in understanding the relationships of these buildings to the liturgy. First, there is great variety in the shape and architecture. We have not touched on the vast central space at Liverpool which lends itself to a great variety of different patterns of worship. We have not reflected on the remarkable classical space, and indeed spaces, offered by St Paul's Cathedral in London. We have not paused at Newcastle, Chelmsford, Wakefield, Portsmouth, or Blackburn, where re-orderings at different times in the last half-century or more have afforded new possibilities in the flexibility of liturgical use with stational rites and other variations. The completion of the cathedrals in St Edmundsbury and Portsmouth also offers new challenges and possibilities, and the architectural eccentricities of Sheffield offer their own conundrums. Second, all this suggests that if our cathedrals are effectively sacramental through their purpose in being designed for prayer, worship and adoration, and the proper imaginative ordering of the liturgy, then all cathedrals (and indeed other church buildings) will be enhanced by the preparation of a *liturgical plan*. Such plans will derive from a profound appreciation of the liturgy and of how liturgy and sacrament speak of God in Jesus Christ, and in relation to the particular building, since, as we have seen, no two buildings are "identical".

LITURGICAL PLANS

In recent years, the Cathedrals Fabric Commission for England has required each cathedral to develop its own liturgical plan. The motive behind this requirement was that, initially, requests would be sent for determination for different projects, commissions, and re-orderings which did not appear to take into account any integrated understanding of the building, nor indeed refer to the theological principles which need to be recognized in properly developing the liturgical and other uses of a cathedral. Why place a particular icon there? Why commission a new piece of stained glass in that chapel? Why move that screen or parclose? What impact will the removal of fixed pews have on the building? Responding to these concerns, the Commission now encourages cathedrals to develop a plan in order that any new works can be seen in the light of this broader theological and spatial understanding. Such plans are not to be inflexible straitjackets, nor are they to ignore the noble Anglican tradition of inductive theology. In other words, empirical desiderata, including architecture, limits on space, and other uses of the building, will be part of the logic employed in producing a theological plan. Furthermore, plans are not produced for eternity without the possibility of change and transformation. They will, however, avoid piecemeal and unreflective change in buildings which require sensitive care and nurture if they are to feed spiritually all who come. So liturgy, in this respect, will include how a cathedral is used for pilgrimages in all understandings of that word. It will include, too, an understanding of how the cathedral foundation hopes that visitors may be encouraged to move around a cathedral to best appreciate the building and, whenever possible, to be moved to prayer and worship.

A number of excellent liturgical plans have already been drafted, and it is probably helpful to examine a sample of just three such plans to comprehend better the nature of this process and how buildings, liturgy, pilgrimage, and even the journeyings of more casual visitors can be better understood. There could hardly be a better place from which to start than Leicester Cathedral, which has had something of a "baptism of fire" as it has needed to respond to the exciting but complicating discovery of the remains of King Richard III. Leicester had been working hard on a liturgical plan, however, well before the king was rediscovered beneath the tarmac of a nearby car park. Leicester is a challenging building for a number of reasons. The building, broad from north to south, includes an intriguing archdeacon's court which is interesting historically but difficult to handle in any liturgical re-ordering. The levels in the cathedral are complicated and any changes will require adaptation in column bases. There is a significant amount of work of a high standard by Sir Charles Nicholson, from the first half of the twentieth century but never completed, and difficult again to adjust in re-ordering. Finally, the rediscovery of King Richard III's remains was exciting but needed to be handled so as not to make them into a shrine.

Leicester's first published plan dates from February 2014 and is a model for such plans.[18] It begins with an examination of the nature and purpose of the cathedral and relates this directly to the liturgy. This introduction sets the cathedral in its context historically and geographically. The landscaping of the Cathedral Gardens to the south of the building and the establishment of joint offices for diocese and cathedral, immediately to the west of the cathedral church in a refurbished school building, have helped lead the way. The three key issues directing liturgical needs are: prayer and narrative within the gospel; the cathedral as the focus of the bishop's ministry; and a place providing common ground for the diverse cultures gathered in the city of Leicester. Each of these has to be conceived against the background of a building within which it has not been easy to articulate these principles.

The building developed as a civic church in the Middle Ages and became a cathedral in 1926. The plan surveys the current pattern of services and their consequent liturgical requirements. Other events are mentioned, as is the handling of visitors, including a current preferred visitor route. Following this comprehensive analysis and description, a new vision for the future is set out. Once again, worship patterns are included and each of the spaces is reviewed. The setting of a central altar with a repositioning of the screen also gives space at the east end for a sacrament chapel where the daily office may be said by the core liturgical community, and visitors also be given a space for prayer and reflection. The south aisle is re-ordered to form a baptistry. Superimposed upon this were the requirements for a burial place for the king. This now lies east of the main altar and west of the sacrament chapel. It remains in a clear position on the new visitor route but without becoming a shrine or centre for pilgrimage. Instead it is a tomb fit for a king.

In moving to Durham, one could hardly choose a greater contrast as a cathedral building. Amongst the larger of the mediaeval new foundation Benedictine cathedrals, Durham is one of the two greatest Romanesque ecclesiastical buildings in England, alongside Norwich. Its architecture is monumental with the strong Norman arcading in both nave and presbytery. Many of the original monastic buildings remain, remodelled over the past four centuries, following the Henrician suppression of the monasteries. The ordering of the liturgical vision is again exemplary, beginning with the purpose and place of Durham Cathedral, moving to the liturgical vision, and then setting this within the historical context and the pattern of services.[19] The section on purpose and place begins with six "pillars" or principles. These encompass worship and spirituality; welcome and care; learning, nurture, and formation; outreach and engagement; buildings, treasures, and environment; and finance and stewardship. The worship of Almighty God is seen as pre-eminent. The historical setting of this within a former Benedictine priory is crucial, and the work of William Charles Lake, dean in the final third of the nineteenth century, sets the scene for the modern period. Again, the pattern of services is described alongside the liturgical use of the cathedral and the subsequent ordering of the liturgy. Music and the use of processional and stational liturgies are given a firm place at the climax of the liturgical plan. Durham's challenges are very different to those of Leicester. The clarity of the structure is undeniable, while the challenge is to use this great building to speak as strongly and imaginatively of the gospel, both liturgically and in welcoming visitors. The shrine of Cuthbert in the retro-choir and the tomb of Bede in the Galilee Chapel are essential elements within the liturgical plan.

A third liturgical plan of great imagination and clarity is that of Birmingham Cathedral.[20] Birmingham, like Leicester, was originally an important civic church at the heart of what would eventually become the second city of England. Unlike Leicester, however, Birmingham Cathedral is effectively a "one-roomed building" conceived as a whole by the seventeenth to eighteenth century Baroque architect, Thomas Archer, and consecrated in 1715. The cathedral is more clearly placed at the heart of Birmingham's civic quarter than is Leicester and the chapter has already paid attention to the immediate setting of the cathedral within the city landscape. In this case, the plan begins with definitions of liturgy which are themselves rooted in a theological understanding of sacred space.[21] Thereafter the plan sets out current liturgical practice, which itself is intended to be derivative of both the Christian tradition and of its own context "in the heart of the business and commercial area of Britain's second city".[22] There is set up here a proper tension between the cathedral acting as a focus for God's presence and also as a "crossing place" for the wider community. The cathedral's significance as the seat of the bishop is acknowledged and its significance within the cultural growth of the city is placed alongside this. The service pattern is described, and there follow key sections on the place of music, on healing ministry, special liturgies, and children. Interesting concepts then define the approach to liturgy—worship is seen as theatre and the building as a "liminal space", the gate of heaven.[23] There is perhaps the strongest enunciation here of a proper theological setting to the liturgy which issues directly into aspirations for the liturgical plan, as envisioned by the chapter.

These three examples of a liturgical plan help return us to the focus of this chapter, deliberately styled "Cathedral-Shaped Worship". We have attempted to see what this might mean both with regard to the historical and theological contexts which help define a cathedral, but also to the ways in which the buildings themselves challenge, limit, and inspire liturgy and worship. Leicester, Durham, and Birmingham are very different buildings in character and architecture. They are also set within profoundly contrasting cultural and historical settings: Leicester is at the heart of a vibrantly multi-cultural, multi-religious city; Durham is classically set within the kernel of a mediaeval city, tracing its roots firmly back to the seventh century re-evangelization of these islands and then the conquest of William I; Birmingham is iconic of a different era again—its city reminds us of the dramatic changes wrought by the Industrial Revolution and all that followed. All these factors, and notably in a more secularized culture, mean that cathedrals face complex challenges in understanding and performing the Church's liturgy. These very challenges, however, offer possibilities and a vision of the gospel unparalleled in any other aspect of the life of God's Church.

NOTES

1. Stephen Platten, "Building Sacraments", in *Theology*, Vol. 117, No. 2 (2014), p. 83 (from the abstract).
2. Plans have now (2017) gone forward to end the parish status of this congregation.
3. Ian Atherton, Eric Fernie, Christopher Harper-Bill, and Hassell Smith (eds.), *Norwich Cathedral: Church, City and Diocese, 1096–1996* (Hambledon Press, 1996).
4. B. A. Windeatt (trans.), *The Book of Margery Kempe* (Penguin, 1985, 1994). See, for example, Chapter 26, p. 96. See also Margaret Gallyon, *Margery Kempe of Lynn and Medieval England* (Canterbury Press, 1995), especially pp. 154–156, and 189.
5. Rule of St Benedict.

6. So, for example, William Castleton was the last prior and first dean, albeit dean only for a year. His portrait still hangs in the Deanery.

7. Canterbury Cathedral also hosts a biennial "Benedictine Experience" conference.

8. Cf., for example, Roberta Gilchrist, *Norwich Cathedral Close: The Evolution of the English Cathedral Landscape* (Boydell Press, 2005).

9. For this see George Guiver's classic study of the development of the daily office in Guiver, *Company of Voices: Daily Prayer and the People of God* (SPCK, 1988, revised edn. Canterbury Press, 2001), p. 96 and *ad loc.*

10. See here especially Edward Yarnold SJ, *The Awe-Inspiring Rites of Initiation: The Origins of the RCIA* (2nd edn, Liturgical Press, 1994). Here Yarnold explores the so-called "mystagogical catechisms" used during Lent in the early Church in preparation for baptism at Easter. He sees it also as the origin and basis of RCIA, that is the Roman Catholic "Rite of Christian Initiation of Adults". This so-called catechetical approach has also been adopted within Anglicanism. The *Pilgrim* course is influenced by this (<http://www.pilgrimcourse.org>).

11. Cf. here Platten, "Building Sacraments", especially pp. 86–88. Some of the following argument is reflected in more detail in that article.

12. William Golding, *The Spire* (Faber, 1964).

13. Quoted in Mark Chapman, *Anglican Theology* (T & T Clark, 2012), p. 74.

14. Platten, "Building Sacraments". See especially pp. 90ff.

15. See Stephen Platten and Christopher Lewis (eds.), *Flagships of the Spirit: Cathedrals in Society* (Darton, Longman and Todd, 1998). See especially pp. xi-xii.

16. Cf. The Venerable Bede, trans. Leo Sherley-Price, *Ecclesiastical History of the English People* (Penguin, 1955, revised edn. 1990), p. 92. The church of St Michael, Cornhill in the City of London is but one example. It is built directly above the foundations of the Roman basilica. It is conceivable, although we do not have conclusive evidence, that worship has been happening on this site since the late second century A.D., first of the Roman Emperor and then later of Jesus Christ.

17. Another parallel example is the shrine of St Edward the Confessor in Westminster Abbey. The abbey was, for a short period, the cathedral church of an episcopal see.

18. Leicester Cathedral Liturgical Plan (<http://leicestercathedral.org/wp-content/uploads/2016/07/Leicester-Cathedral-Revealed-Liturgical-Plan.pdf>).

19. Durham Cathedral Liturgical Plan, with copyright to The Chapter of Durham Cathedral.

20. Birmingham Cathedral Liturgy Plan (<http://birminghamcathedral. contentfiles.net/media/assets/file/Birmingham_Cathedral_Liturgy_Plan.pdf>).

21. Birmingham Cathedral Liturgy Plan.

22. Here cf. again John Inge, *A Christian Theology of Place* (Ashgate, 2003), *ad loc.*

23. Birmingham Cathedral Liturgy Plan, p. 6, section 3.1.

6. FURNISHINGS

Jane Kennedy

TRANSCENDENT SPACE

The furnishing of British cathedrals is rich and diverse. In this chapter I hope to examine how furnishings affect our experience of these buildings. I will ask whether furnishings are necessary and then look at what furnishings say in major churches. Do they help the visitor to understand that this is a place of worship? Should they? And if so, how do we reconcile this with the diversity of events now occurring in many buildings? And finally, I will suggest an approach to the design of new furnishings in cathedrals.

> Everywhere there was but little furniture, and that only the most necessary and of the simplest forms. The extravagant love of ornament which I had noted in this people elsewhere seemed here to have given place to the feeling that the house itself and its associations was the ornament of the country life of which it had been left stranded from old times, and that to re-ornament it would but take away its use as a piece of natural beauty.[1]

William Morris's love for simple interiors has had a deep impact on our enjoyment of historic buildings and informed both the Arts and Crafts and Modern movements in architecture and design. His ideas have remained relevant throughout the twentieth and twenty-first centuries, and not only for the domestic interior. Imagine arriving in a great mediaeval cathedral such as Lincoln, where the nave is usually cleared of furnishings. The sight is glorious, a vision of the Heavenly Jerusalem to which furniture could contribute very little of significance. For many people an uncluttered interior and a powerful sense of scale, space, mystery, and architectural grandeur are what our cathedrals are all about.

There is no immediate view of an altar in Lincoln nave and very little in the way of religious paraphernalia. At Ely, where the nave is sometimes cleared of chairs—accentuating not only the majesty of its architecture but also revealing Gilbert Scott's splendid paving—a foreign visitor was once heard to ask, "Is this place still used?" The ability to rearrange or clear these majestic spaces ought to be a key requirement of any furnishing scheme with all that implies in terms of storage and mobility. Often the naves of our Anglican cathedrals are furnished for secular events: a concert with staging, even chairs and tables for a business dinner, or they will simply be full of schoolchildren experiencing life as monks. We often need to explore further, by passing through a stone screen perhaps, to encounter a sanctuary and to understand that this is a building still used for worship. The ritual quire may be raised up a flight of steps; it will be subtly lit and perhaps enclosed by screens and stalls. A space which is cosy and reassuring for the confident worshipper at Evensong but perhaps exclusive for visitors; you can peer in but are you allowed to enter?

What the visitor experiences on coming into a modern Roman Catholic cathedral is subtly different. Entering through the glass doors and into the narthex of Clifton Cathedral, your eye will immediately be taken to the pool of light over the altar. Taken past orderly rows of seats, a wall of coloured glass, and the font and baptistry chapel to a formal open space flooded with white light, and on to the sanctuary. The experience is similarly dramatic at Liverpool Metropolitan Cathedral, where the visitor immediately fixes on the central altar lit by a lantern of coloured glass, and with carefully laid-out bench seating through three hundred and sixty degrees. The purpose of these buildings is immediately obvious and the furnishings invite participation in worship. Both these cathedrals, Liverpool by Sir Frederick Gibberd, built between 1962 and 1967, and Clifton, by the Percy Thomas Partnership between 1969 and 1973, were responses to changes in liturgy made lawful in the Second Vatican Council and subsequent measures including the new Roman Missal 1969 which confirmed that:

> The altar should be built apart from the wall, in such a way that it is possible to walk around it easily and that Mass can be celebrated at it facing the people, which is desirable wherever possible.[2]

HISTORY AND DEVELOPMENT

When thinking about the furnishings of these great buildings it is important to understand their history and the developments in liturgy and use which have resulted in changes to their interiors. Several English mediaeval cathedrals started life as monastic churches where monks worshipped in an enclosed choir at the centre of the building. The monks had their own altar and, beyond a further screen, the space for the high altar. There were usually a significant number of side and eastern chapels, shrines, and chantries. Secular cathedrals would have had provision for canons, similarly using an enclosed choir, and Lincoln exemplifies this. There would be up to three altars at the eastern end of the nave (themselves protected by screens), for local parishes and the laity in general. In the late Middle Ages the eastern parts of cathedrals were filled with liturgical furnishings, statuary, textiles, and paintings but little or nothing in the way of congregational seating in the nave. A great deal of this art and furniture was removed after the Reformation. In the centuries which followed, the liturgy became simpler and there were fewer services, although choir stalls were retained to become seating areas for dean and chapter, bishop, and choir. Worship centred on an eastern high altar.

All of this was reworked and often richly embellished in the nineteenth century. At the same time, with the need to create new dioceses to serve expanding populations, large parish churches were designated cathedrals and adapted to emulate their mediaeval predecessors. This involved major reordering or additions. For example, at Newcastle, when England's largest parish church became a cathedral in 1882, it required no extension. Instead, a new set piece and enclosed choir,[3] with highly decorative woodwork and sculpture, was created east of the crossing to house high altar, clergy, and singers.

In the nineteenth and twentieth centuries, there have also been new purpose-built cathedrals in areas where there were no adequate early buildings to convert. Truro incorporates a small late-mediaeval aisle but is otherwise an entirely new creation, as is Liverpool Anglican Cathedral; both were laid out and furnished imaginatively, broadly based on historical precedents. The twentieth century saw some new cathedral buildings with fully designed and integrated furnishings.

If we are to commission and design new furnishings for cathedrals, we need to understand how they have adapted to change. At Ely, in the eighteenth century, the stone pulpitum was removed from the nave and the choir stalls were moved from their original position under the octagon to the east end of the choir. Services were few, if regular, and the Eucharist became less important. In the early nineteenth century, a small congregation worshipped in the choir each Sunday. They came out and moved west into the nave where they were joined by members of other congregations in the city, sometimes bringing their own seats, to hear the sermon, after which the small cathedral congregation returned to the choir for the end of their service.

The mid-nineteenth century liturgical developments in the Anglican Church brought about further significant changes. When Gilbert Scott was employed to repair and re-order the building at Ely, he moved the stalls back to the western bays of the choir with a fine new screen and pulpit. The congregation now sat on bench seats in the octagon, the clergy and musicians in their stalls. Scott re-used a little over half of the mediaeval stalls in the new choir.[4]

In the mid-twentieth century, distaste for things Victorian coincided with re-ordering in both Anglican and Catholic churches following the lead given by the Second Vatican Council. Some furnishings were lost—Scott's fine screens at Hereford and Salisbury were removed.[5] The widespread introduction of nave altars was carried out with varying degrees of success. At Ely, George Pace was commissioned to design new furnishings. His new altar in the octagon became the focus of Sunday worship for a congregation now largely gathered in the transept and the nave. Pace, in the twentieth century, made changes in buildings almost as extensively as Scott in the nineteenth. His finest work, at Llandaff Cathedral and the nearby chapel at St Michael's College, has great integrity, and there is no doubt that he studied and understood the mediaeval architecture with which he worked at a profound level. At Southwark, his furnishings are almost ubiquitous and create an impressive modern ensemble. They are, however, replicated in many other churches and cathedrals and so cannot be rooted in an understanding of the particular place. At Ely, Pace adapted his "standard" designs for altar, platform, and clergy seats and stalls under the octagon. To this ensemble were added, after Pace's death, less elegant choir stalls. Pace's work uses light oak and although the seating is quirky, altar, platform, and kneeling benches are very plain and simple.

The arrangement under the octagon at Ely works very well. In other places with a smaller crossing, the dilemma is whether the nave altar should be under the crossing and thus a little separate from the nave or brought west into the nave with the problem of a north-south route between it and the choir. Many nave altars in Anglican cathedrals look temporary because they need to be moveable for concert staging. The more permanent arrangements in the Roman Catholic Church intentionally preclude most secular uses and are often more successful aesthetically and liturgically. The resolution of this dilemma in the Anglican context requires ingenuity and sensitivity.

More recent liturgical developments have encouraged a fuller use of buildings during the Eucharist, with a service starting in the nave and progressing eastwards into the choir. The rebuilding of Portsmouth Cathedral by the architect Michael Drury, responding to the ideas of David Stancliffe when Provost, was its first working out, developed further by Richard Giles in Philadelphia.[6] Both schemes engage the congregation fully in the service and contrast with the more standard cathedral service where the congregation sits in rows as an audience. Movement is often resisted by elderly members of congregations who prefer to remain seated, and by clergy who feel nervous about how all this is to be managed. But movement through great spaces is engaging and processions both within and around great churches have significant historical precedents. At Ely, processions sometimes begin in the Lady Chapel where the standing congregation naturally feels more involved and alert. This sense of engagement is central to worship in the Russian Orthodox Church where standing and moving about is normal. It combines drama and informality as well as the sense that the service is a kind of mobile continuum that may be joined at any stage.

LITURGY, MYSTERY, FURNISHING

So do we need furnishings? If the answer is "Yes" there is a strong argument for using simple designs and avoiding clutter, and thus confusion. A building full of pews will not enable movement or experiments in liturgy and performance. If the splendour of our mediaeval cathedrals is most fully realised when the naves are empty of furniture, and if congregations feel more involved when standing and moving, what furnishings do we need? Certainly an altar, ambo, and a minimum of three clergy seats if the most frequent celebrations are not at the high altar; probably some choir stalls which can be moveable to allow experimentation with music; and some comfortable and moveable or stackable seats. Clearing space will often mean the removal of some existing furnishings. There is a consensus that decisions about removing, disposing of, or storing furnishings must be informed by an understanding of their history and significance.[7] It is unlikely that permission would be given today to remove a Scott screen because we now value his work more highly, but the removal of banks of Victorian pews, seen as an obstacle both to liturgical change and to the introduction of wider community and arts events, will often be allowed. Large sets of pews are unlikely to find new homes and "sample" pews are often kept as a reminder of how buildings were furnished. Redundant altars, lecterns, and pulpits are more problematic: the nave triforium at Ely has, in common, doubtless, with many other cathedrals, a bulky collection of nineteenth and twentieth-century liturgical furnishings which may never be used again.

Modern congregational seating must be comfortable and, given the challenge of designing comfortable chairs, it is unlikely that this will be devised satisfactorily on an individual basis. Indeed there is now plenty of evidence that catalogue pews were introduced widely in nineteenth-century parish churches.[8] The most successful modern solution has been the Howe 40/4 chair whose simplicity, lightness, and stacking capability have made it a popular choice in several cathedrals. Other good modern designs have followed, such as Chorus Furniture's "Theo" chair, and what both lack in individuality is more than compensated by their relatively low visual impact. It will be worth exploring the potential for using modern materials for chairs which have even less visual impact yet are comfortable and very easy to stack.

There needs to be a balance in these great buildings between focusing on the arrangement for the liturgy and on the means by which we advise and guide visitors. Anglican cathedral chapters will emphasize the importance of worship at the heart of what they do, but the space is often adapted to provide for tourists (pilgrims?) through interpretive facilities, welcome and pay desks, and perhaps shop fittings and display cases. All "furnishings", whether temporary or permanent, affect our experience of these buildings. Notice boards advertising events and services distract, but simple information and wayfinding are necessary. Uncluttered entrances make arrival easy, and ticketing, purchase of guide books, audio guides and so on should probably take place where this will not obstruct views or distract from the dramatic experience of entering a great architectural and liturgical space. Even on the busiest of days, visitors should feel welcomed, and good furnishings can help to orientate and guide them to understand the purpose of the building and to find the focus of worship.

A cathedral visit can be a profound experience in the early morning or on a dark winter afternoon when low lighting and perhaps the sound of a choir rehearsing will direct and draw us through the space. As curators of these buildings, we must ensure that our activities and our busyness are not made less visible by unnecessary clutter which can destroy that experience.

Wayfinding, outside and inside the building, should be clear and simply marked. It should be consistent throughout the cathedral and its precinct, and not mixed up with posters and other notices. It needs to go hand in hand with careful lighting to help us find our way through the building safely and to guide us to key monuments and architectural features and spaces. Natural light is infinitely variable and should be enjoyed; artificial light must be added subtly and should generally behave like daylight: that is to say, to fall from above. Uplights have their uses, particularly for vaulting and decorative ceilings, but they can also create unhappy effects; mouldings and other architectural details were designed to throw shadows downwards. Similarly, lighting needs to be restricted to fall where needed; on the congregation's hymn books, for example, but not flooding walls and seating areas so that definition and excitement is lost.

A WORKED EXAMPLE

It is instructive to understand how recent changes at Ely Cathedral have been commissioned and developed. The starting place when considering commissioning furnishings, art, or fittings must be a thorough understanding of the architectural and liturgical history of the place. Essential in guiding change is the drawing up of a "liturgical plan" by the chapter with advice from its architect. This document explains how the building is currently used for worship throughout the Christian year, what happens at festivals, and what is the chapter's vision for future developments in liturgy.

The best work is likely to emerge from working with (and not against) the building. At Ely, where I have worked for many years, I have tried to make additions which, though clearly new, sit discretely within and alongside the historic fabric. Thus, the addition of a link between the choir and Lady Chapel, on the footprint of its long disappeared mediaeval predecessor, was built in a very simple late-mediaeval Gothic style developed from the elevations of the early sixteenth-century cloister. It is embellished by the glazing designed with Keith Barley and gilded bosses made by Peter Eugene Ball. Both use traditional forms and iconography but add real interest to the interior. The achievement of a seamless transition between two magnificent historic interiors relies on a relatively self-effacing addition that many visitors pass through without remark.

This passage enters the Lady Chapel on its south side and through two mediaeval doors. The chapel, having become a parish church after the Reformation and then returned to the cathedral in the mid-twentieth century, had been stripped of furnishings with a modern quarry tile floor laid. With its vast windows, it was also a very cold building and we could lay a new floor, with underfloor heating to allow the building to be used throughout the year. With scant knowledge of the mediaeval floor design and only a few squares of Purbeck marble left as evidence, the richness of mediaeval floor patterns (well understood by Scott in his paving of the nave and choir) informed designs in new Purbeck stones.

The subsequent controversial introduction to the chapel of a brightly painted statue of the Virgin by David Wynne posed a challenging problem more recently for the design of a new reredos and altar in the chapel. The commission was undertaken by the architectural historian and artist John Maddison. He has explained how the ideas behind his design sit within the building in a way which exemplifies both understanding of the place and a creative theological response to the chapel:

> The original purpose of the building was to celebrate the intercessory power of the Virgin and to provide a spectacular setting for the liturgy associated with her. It was completed in the middle of the fourteenth century but the sanctuary was altered in the late fourteenth century by the introduction of an elaborate painted and carved reredos. Iconoclasm in the Tudor period and in the Civil War destroyed the 147 sculptures which decorated the chapel inside and out and defaced the remarkable dado reliefs illustrating the life and miracles of the Virgin. The mediaeval reredos lost its thirteen small figures and was further damaged in around 1700 when a baroque oak altarpiece with text panels was fixed to the east wall.
>
> The new scheme balances the Marian devotion which David Wynne's statue encourages, with an indication of the figure's significance as a symbol of the Incarnation. In

all this it was also very important to have due regard for
the Reformation history of the building and the religious
convictions of the reformers who deprived the chapel of
its mediaeval imagery. It was also important to do nothing
by way of new art work that might distract attention from
the quiet voice of the painted mediaeval decoration that
survives at the east end and the remarkable beauty of the
chapel as a whole.

The design makes the whole altar platform more usable
liturgically by clearing it of unnecessary furniture. It includes
a fine wrought-iron screen set in front of the late-fourteenth-
century stone reredos, so arranged that it conceals some of
the damage and restores a feeling of coherence and dignity
to this beautiful but battered object. The metal screen
supports a canopy made entirely of metal letters in place
of the lost projecting canopy of the mediaeval reredos.
This is very much a contemporary design, but it makes
reference to mediaeval and post-Reformation metalwork
without copying specific historic detail. The letters of the
name MARIA are arranged like ciphers so that they are not
easily legible but read rather as ornament.

The altar is composed of the oak slab of the former altar.
The supporting trestles of wrought iron frame a panel of
thick, gilded sheet steel pierced through with an inscription
composed from the first chapter of John. In this design the
word upholds the sacrament. In describing the Incarnation,
it gives meaning to the statue and by referring specifically to
the word, to truth and to grace it speaks of the foundations
of our Anglican Communion.[9]

INTEGRITY AND DESIGN

How does craftsmanship contribute to the integrity of furnishings? Chris Topp's wrought ironwork in the Lady Chapel at Ely contributes through its detailing and construction to the delight of the work. We often feel that the beauty of mediaeval and Renaissance church furnishings derives from the skill of the individual craftsmen but that it was also given integrity by their personal faith. We do not find this in later, more mass-produced furnishings, even where they were hand-made. The nineteenth-century pews at Newcastle, for example, were obviously hand-made, with craftsmen reproducing a small set of designs by Ralph Hedley, but there was no scope for the individual interpretation seen in similar mediaeval work. Does this matter?

I think it does, but there are relatively few examples in contemporary religious architecture and design. If we look to other areas of the arts we can see, for example, how the conviction and integrity of such composers as John Tavener and James MacMillan have produced outstanding contributions to church music, and we are profoundly challenged and engaged by the video installations of Bill Viola. Must we accept that, without a continuing and developing tradition of the kind exemplified by mediaeval sculptors or nineteenth-century metalworkers, we will not see much that is fine or beautiful added to our cathedrals in our time? I hope not, but we should set high standards and demand of the designers of furnishings an engagement with the buildings, with theology, and with liturgy. The finest contemporary example of such engagement is Niall McLaughlin's chapel for Ripon College, Cuddesdon. Here the integrated design of the building and furnishings creates a quiet but stimulating space for students, visitors, and the religious community. It is not, of course, a cathedral. We can, however, look to William Pye's font at Salisbury. Pye has the skill of an artist who understands both elemental forces and place, and his font delights and challenges as do the best of our historic cathedral furnishings. It is simple and beautiful in its detailing and construction. Rather than do a great thing badly it will be better to do a small thing well.

NOTES

1. William Morris, *News from Nowhere* (Penguin, 1998), p. 221.
2. General Instruction of the Roman Missal (GIRM), p. 299.
3. The architect was R. L. Johnson and the woodwork was designed by Ralph Hedley.
4. The remaining seats were dismantled and stored in the triforium where they remain, catalogued, recorded, and shelved today.
5. The Hereford screen can be enjoyed in the Victoria and Albert Museum.
6. Richard Giles, *Creating Uncommon Worship: Transforming the Liturgy of the Eucharist* (Canterbury Press, 2004).
7. A formal guidance note is in the course of preparation by the Cathedrals Fabric Commission for England at the time of writing.
8. Trevor Cooper and Sarah Brown (eds.), *Pews, Benches and Chairs: Church Seating in English Parish Churches from the Fourteenth Century to the Present* (The Ecclesiological Society, 2011).
9. Unpublished artist's statement, 2016.

7. *SOSTENUTO CON BRIO*

Richard Shephard

CATHEDRAL MUSIC—FOR WHOM?

There are two very important questions concerning contemporary cathedral music: for whom is the music, and is the tradition sustainable?

To begin with the first question—"For whom is cathedral music?" Clearly from the earliest times music has been used as an adjunct to worship. Miriam sang her song to the Lord; David the Psalmist wrote lyrics for works of praise, for supplication, for mourning; the writer of the Epistle to the Ephesians mentions psalms, hymns, and spiritual songs. So there is a lengthy biblical tradition of music as an essential part of religious life. What we do not know, however, is of what sort the music was, whether it broke new artistic ground, if it appealed to the whole worshipping community or merely to a few aficionados. But we can probably assume—based on knowledge of western music for the last thousand years or so—that there was not the variety of styles that are present in today's musical world. And it is this great variety which poses a challenge for those who are responsible for music in cathedrals.

At the present time there are many different elements in music nationally: pop music, theatrical musicals, classical repertoire, modern or avant-garde classical music, evangelical choruses, grand opera . . . to name but a few. So possibly the question should be asked as to which style or styles might be most fitting for the worship of God in a cathedral.

Let us look at the cathedral tradition first, and the music which the majority of worshippers would immediately associate with cathedrals. The tradition broadly dates from composers such as William Byrd, Thomas Tallis, and Orlando Gibbons, developing through John Blow, Henry Purcell, and Pelham Humfrey, then on to William Boyce, William Croft, William Crotch, and into the nineteenth century which was possibly a low point, with the exception of such composers as Jonathan Battishill, Samuel Sebastian Wesley, and (arguably) Sir John Stainer. There then followed the English musical renaissance, and leaving aside Edward Elgar and Hubert Parry, composers like Charles Villiers Stanford and Charles Wood—both extremely competent—helped to build on and add to the tradition. Into the twentieth century, things become slightly more confusing. This is because classical music developed in many different ways. The impressionist style was still able to provide enjoyment to quite a wide audience, and possibly the English composer who assimilated at least some of these stylistic features was Herbert Howells, whose music has retained a strong hold on the cathedral repertoire. Then there was the folk-song tradition, carefully researched by Vaughan Williams. His editing of the music for the *English Hymnal* was certainly a pivotal moment in Anglican worship generally. Since the early twentieth century, however, cathedral music has been faced with a number of challenges and opportunities: not merely in the choice of repertoire but also in the manner of performance.

Arguably the most important change in performance has been the addition of girls' choirs to the musical establishment. Salisbury Cathedral Choir, under the direction of Richard Seal, was the first establishment to create parallel choirs of boys and girls. Many other cathedrals have followed suit and this has been of benefit in many ways. Girls are certainly capable of singing as well as boys, and the tone quality of each choir is largely the result of the musical direction. One has only to compare the boys' choirs of two Cambridge colleges, King's and St John's, to realise that there is not one generic sound for boys and, hence, the same applies to girls. And of course, even if girls did sound markedly different, would that matter? Choirs are there for the worship of God, and one cannot imagine the Almighty turning off the celestial transistor radio merely because the choir was female rather than male.

Another obvious change has been the manner of performance in cathedral services. In the first half of the twentieth century—and in some places for years beyond—conductors appeared very infrequently. The cathedral organist played for the services and the choir looked after itself. Sometimes a chorister might nod across to the opposite side, sometimes lay clerks on each side would keep a discreet beat going to ensure that all held together. Nowadays the norm is for the organist to conduct everything. Some manage to do this in a discreet manner; others can provide a rather unpleasant distraction as they gyrate and gesture, sometimes in the middle of the choir.

MUSICAL GENRES

Next we could consider the music which characterizes the worship in many evangelical churches. In contrast to the so-called cathedral tradition, it has tended to favour worship songs and to do away with traditional accompaniment, replacing the organ with an amplified band such as is used in some pop music. There can be a feeling that the provision of worship songs, accompanied by an amplified band, could help to attract more worshippers to cathedrals, but there are two distinct challenges in so doing: the acoustics and general ambience of ancient cathedrals do not readily lend themselves to informal worship, to amplified singers or instrumentalists. (There is also a reasonable question as to why a primitive Spanish folk instrument—the guitar—should be perceived as remotely appropriate to English liturgy.) But perhaps more important is the fairly obvious fact that worship songs could well discourage existing cathedral congregational members from attendance, largely because they have musical and liturgical tastes which differ widely from such evangelical worship. There is another very important challenge when dealing with music which is outside the cathedral tradition: there can be a danger that the music is perceived as a performance for which the players and singers could be applauded—and this does happen in some churches. While it is perfectly acceptable to attend concerts of church music, and appropriate to applaud the performers, that is certainly not the case in matters liturgical. Services of worship are for the glory of God, not for the adulation of singers and instrumentalists. On the same subject, there has been a recent trend in some cathedrals to applaud organ voluntaries. Members of the congregation are often encouraged not to talk during concluding voluntaries, which are perceived as the finishing of the liturgical event; so again, there is a degree of inappropriateness in applauding the voluntary, as there would be if members of the congregation decided to applaud the anthem or even—however unlikely—the sermon.

Contemporary so-called classical music is in a somewhat fragmented state: unlike music in earlier centuries there is no one main path which serious composers are following. There are some who attempt to build on the traditions, and others who see it as important to branch out in different ways. One has only to compare the compositions of Karlheinz Stockhausen, John Tavener, Steve Reich, and Arvo Pärt to see that there is a somewhat bemusing plethora of styles. It is, of course, impossible to predict which music, if any, will survive for a century or even for a few decades. What clearly *is* important is that composers should remember that music written for the liturgy needs to assist worshippers and not alienate them. So it can be somewhat condescending if composers look upon it as their task to write music principally to educate congregations and to display their own musical wares. The following note was written in 1978 by composer Jonathan Harvey, who had been commissioned to write a setting of the evening canticles for the Southern Cathedrals Festival in Winchester:

> Anyone who knows both the world of avant-garde music and the world of Anglican church music cannot fail to be struck by the sad fact that much exciting music of spiritual import hasn't a hope of entering those time-honoured and notoriously conservative portals. Or has it? The vision of our great cathedrals as once again the spearhead of all that is adventurous, imaginative and sacred in our torn culture helped me write this piece, by no means "adventurous" by avant-garde standards, but certainly exploiting vocal

possibilities rarely if ever encountered in liturgical Anglican
Evening Canticles before. It embodies a hope.[1]

What exactly was the hope that Harvey stated was embodied in his
Magnificat and *Nunc Dimittis*? The hope of regular future performances?
The hope of many avant-garde pieces in all cathedral repertoires? The hope
of appealing to a large liturgical audience? The hope of altering once and
for all the evolutionary way in which cathedral music has built gradually
on historical traditions? If any of the above were his hopes, they have all
been dashed to the ground.

What all composers need to understand and accept is that providing
music for the liturgy will inevitably lead to a degree of compromise. It is
important not to be patronizing, but equally important to provide music
of a quality—both written and performed—which assists worship and
is appropriate to its historical and architectural setting. The survival of
particular anthems and canticles into the future is in no way connected
with the effort put into composing or the attempts, no matter how
sincere, to be at the forefront of contemporary classical composition: it
is up to succeeding generations to make a judgement, and it is important
to recognize that the majority of church music which has been written
over the last couple of centuries has been consigned to the eternal waste
bin. And there is nothing intrinsically wrong with this: liturgical music
is there for a purpose, and once it no longer fulfils that purpose it has
outlived its usefulness.

SCOPE OF CATHEDRAL MUSIC

So, in the twenty-first century, to what extent can cathedral liturgy be "all
things to all people"? To what extent should attempts be made to reach
differing sectors of the worshipping community if adopting certain styles
alienates a percentage of the congregation? How should music be chosen?
It is easy to see that those who are given the responsibility for choosing
liturgical music are bound to be constrained by their own tastes, their

own knowledge of the complete repertoire, and possibly the whims of other colleagues, clerical or lay. There are many conflicting pressures to do with the musical elements within liturgy. Most important to remember is that music is there to enhance worship, not to be a free-standing concert item. In that cathedral worship has grown in popularity over the decades, it is clearly important to cherish the centuries-old choral tradition and to build on that, rather than to attempt to revolutionize. If cathedrals, then, are to continue to encourage the production of new liturgical music, it is increasingly important that composers should be given a very clear brief as to what is required. Many commissioned works have, over the last fifty years or so, been given a first and only performance. This is not only a waste of a commission fee, but it also implies that the work did not fulfil liturgical needs. So commissioning bodies have a responsibility for making clear what is required, and composers have a responsibility for following that brief.

Given modern technology, social media such as Facebook and Twitter, and more traditional broadcasting, new commissions can receive much more publicity than was the case twenty or thirty years ago. Publishers have modernized their marketing strategies considerably, and there has been a trend, begun in North America, to persuade churches to sign up to a system which enables them, for an annual subscription, to download music from the Internet. This is certainly an innovative idea, meaning that churches and cathedrals can study potential new repertoire items without having to go to the expense and trouble of buying a hard copy.

IS CATHEDRAL MUSIC SUSTAINABLE?

Our second important question is, "Is cathedral music sustainable?" Over the years many professional musicians have begun their careers as choristers in one of the great cathedral or collegiate choirs. In the last twenty-five years or so this path to a professional career has been available to girls as well as boys and there are growing numbers of female members of the music profession who have been choristers. There is an obvious financial issue in the business of running a cathedral choir. Of course, there are different models: some cathedrals run choirs as a totally voluntary exercise; others will pay the lay clerks (lay vicars, songmen, singing men) and will also provide scholarships for the choristers to attend independent choir schools. But even those cathedrals which run voluntary choirs will have considerable expenses in buying music, in buying robes, in paying organists. Perhaps the important thing to remember is that all cathedrals were built as places of worship, and that worship is absolutely at the heart of cathedral life. Members of the governing bodies of cathedrals tend to be in post for comparatively short periods of time, and during their short tenure of office they have a responsibility for keeping these historic buildings in good repair and maintaining a high standard of worship. Given the lack of financial support centrally from the Church of England or from central government, this is a frightening burden to bear. Despite this, however, there can be a temptation for some of them to wish to leave a legacy—by installing a new chapel; by buying works of art; by pursuing personal theological or evangelistic interests—all of which may well be worthy and laudable, but may also be a drain on ever-diminishing finances which have to ensure the continuity of worship inside expensively maintained historic buildings.

Another source of anxiety when considering the sustainability of the precious tradition of cathedral music is the recruitment of singers, both adults and children. The old system of employing lay clerks has been eroded over many years. Many cathedrals now have young choral scholars to fill places on the back row. This can be excellent for many reasons: choral scholars tend to come from universities and colleges in the same region as the cathedral. Having young men in the choir from age eighteen to twenty-one or twenty-two gives a superb opportunity for cathedrals to provide education, not merely musically, but in the area of liturgy both modern and historical. It is vitally important that there is an understanding that the term "choral scholarship" has a deep implication that the scholars will receive an education from the cathedral. It must never be perceived as a system which allows for the employment of young people at a significantly cheaper rate than lay clerks.

Recruitment of lay clerks can be more difficult. Singing daily services, and possibly three or four services at the weekend, is a considerable commitment for those with full-time jobs and families. Additionally, from the cathedral's viewpoint, if someone is appointed in his forties, then the likelihood is that there will be little vocal improvement over succeeding decades, and probably the reverse.

With regard to the recruitment of choristers, there is a growing problem over the commitment to singing at many daily services and possibly having shorter holidays than other children. There has been a decline in boarding numbers of children at ages seven to thirteen which has inevitably meant that cathedral choristerships are largely available only to those children whose families reside in reasonable proximity to a cathedral, and whose parents are able to manage the complicated and demanding timetable of fetching and carrying to and from the services and rehearsals. General expectations of chorister life have changed markedly in the last half-century. At Gloucester Cathedral, for example, in the 1950s and 1960s, choir members were allowed only two Sundays off each year. This meant that choristers could have a three-week break around the two middle Sundays in August. There were days off after Christmas and Easter, but no other Sundays. At that time there were far fewer recreational and occupational opportunities for children, so the timetable was accepted as the norm. This would clearly be unacceptable nowadays, and even given the concept of shorter terms, longer holidays, and fewer services, the pace of life and the many conflicting pressures on families has meant that parents have to consider very carefully the implications of signing up to five years or so of chauffeuring their children to rehearsals and services. But, of course, a choristership offers a unique educational experience. At a very early age, children perform music to a professional level; they learn the importance of relating to other members of the team; they learn to concentrate and to stand still and, through services and concerts, they become acquainted with a wide choral repertoire. So there needs to be clarity in making known what it is that cathedrals are offering educationally to both children and young adults.

Having mentioned singers in cathedrals, we now come on to a somewhat more contentious aspect of cathedral music, namely the people who direct the choirs. Possibly for financial reasons cathedrals have, historically, employed an organist. This person played the organ and, as mentioned earlier, the choir generally looked after itself. When looked at logically, and in the context of contemporary practice, there does seem to be something rather eccentric in this system. Playing the organ is perhaps the most independent of all musical activities. The instrument is complete in itself and the skills involved in playing it are as different as possible from those that are required for playing in an orchestra or singing in an ensemble. Recently there have been one or two appointments in which the director of the choir is not necessarily an organist, but rather someone who has experience of what it is to be a singer. Of course there have also, over the years, been many organists who have been extremely competent at both playing the organ and also directing a choir. Equally, however, there have been (historically) a number of cathedrals in which this has not been the case.

Career paths for cathedral directors of music are few and narrow. There is little mobility in the system, and becoming a cathedral musician can be perceived as driving into a professional cul-de-sac. Historically, cathedral organists have tended to stay in post for a significant number of years. Samuel Sebastian Wesley, who held posts at Winchester College, Hereford Cathedral, Exeter Cathedral, Winchester Cathedral, and Gloucester Cathedral, was an interesting exception. In the present world of employment, however, young people are being told that they should not expect to remain in the same role for the whole of their working life. There are several elements that militate against more fluidity and flexibility in the world of cathedral organists: many (but not all) post-holders enjoy the comfort of large historic houses in attractive cities; some are able to benefit from a full-time salary for what can be, in effect, a part-time job with extremely generous holidays; interestingly there have been few, if any, cases in which the performance of the director of music has been appraised regularly. Appraisal of a cathedral musician presents problems as to who the appraiser should be; it would be no more appropriate for a dean to appraise a choral conductor than it would be for the conductor to appraise the dean's preaching. So clearly this presents a challenge. Appraisal by a fellow cathedral organist would be ineffectual: it would be unlikely for one musical incumbent to recommend the termination of another's contract for fear that something similar might be done to him or her.

PROFESSIONAL DEVELOPMENT

In all areas of employment there is a danger in incumbents staying too long. The world of cathedral music is, by its nature, traditional and conforms to an unchanging liturgical pattern. Within that pattern there is a small amount of elbow room for development but there is, rightly, a limit on innovation, which means that after ten, twenty, thirty years or more there can be a degree of stagnation. Of course, there have been several very distinguished musicians who have maintained a high standard for decades, but these have been the exception rather than the rule. In general terms, members of chapters serve for fewer years than many organists and it is easy to see that an incoming dean would find it almost impossible to dismiss a musician, no matter how ineffectual, who might have been in post for over twenty years. So there remains a challenge which has to do not only with the standard of music in a cathedral but also with fostering a musician's career development. Is there any way that a cathedral musician's career could be developed? It is easy to see the traditional path from assistant to director in a small cathedral, then on to a larger enterprise, but the path is narrow and the opportunities are few. In that a substantial part of the life of a director of choristers is in effect being a teacher of children, perhaps research could be done into the possibilities of directors coming from or going to schools. Part of the job is to do with administration, so perhaps there might also be openings in the wider world of professional music. When addressing the whole area of musicians' career development, thought needs to be given to the whole music profession and not solely to the excellent but inevitably restricted world of cathedrals. How this could all be brought about is somewhat problematic, so perhaps it is time for another Cathedrals' Commission to review the present situation and to make radical proposals which will recommend best practice to institutions.[2]

THE FUTURE

The world of choral music has altered and developed very rapidly over the last fifty years or so. The Clerkes of Oxenford, The Sixteen, The Tallis Scholars, I Fagiolini, Tenebrae . . . there are countless professional choirs which now sing (among other things) music from the cathedral repertoire, so there are a number of openings for choral conductors. Perhaps as the century proceeds there may be more opportunities for talented musicians to move in and out of the cathedral world, thereby refreshing the worlds of both liturgical and concert music.

The standard of cathedral music has arguably never been higher. It is important for there to be a realization nationally of the uniqueness of religious and musical life, and of how England leads the world in this area of cultural expertise. The maintenance of cathedral music will become no less expensive, and if the cathedral world is to attract musicians of the highest calibre and to commission new and appropriate works for the enhancement of the liturgy, then inevitably costs will rise. Many cathedrals are building up funds to ensure the continuation of their choirs. Various national institutions, such as the Friends of Cathedral Music, give financial support, but these systems are, to a certain extent, a hand-to-mouth measure for keeping things going. The unique cultural treasure of cathedral music is something which merits national support. How this might be brought about needs thought and discussion with a degree of urgency since, if the system begins to fail for financial reasons, it would be very difficult to breathe new life into it.

From Samuel Sebastian Wesley until the present day there have been writings about the challenges facing cathedral music. Evidence implies that cathedral congregations are growing, while congregations in parishes are dwindling. There could be many reasons for both growth and shrinkage, but one of the main attractions of cathedral worship is its music. The challenges nowadays (unlike those of Wesley's time) are not so much concerned with standards: broadcasting, social media, and general networking have ensured that everyone can recognize what a good choir should sound like, so standards are high and are set to continue so. Possibly the greatest challenge will be finance. There are more pressures on chapters than in the whole of history: the expense of running cathedrals, keeping ancient buildings in good repair, conforming to legislation concerning health and safety, employment practice, safeguarding, and a host of other matters mean that costs inevitably rise. What must always be remembered is that, without the best possible standard of worship within these historic buildings, the core purpose of cathedrals has been pushed aside, and the buildings become no more than tourist attractions.

NOTES

1. In the programme note to his *Magnificat* and *Nunc Dimittis* in the 1978 Southern Cathedrals Festival programme.
2. In April 2017 the Archbishops of Canterbury and York set up a Cathedrals Working Group to review aspects of cathedral management and governance, but music was not a specific part of its remit.

8.   CATHEDRALS AT PRAYER

Peter Atkinson

THE NATURE OF PRAYER

It is an axiom of Christian theology that all prayer is offered to God the Father, in the power of the Holy Spirit, and in union with Jesus Christ. The only one who prays perfectly is Christ the great high priest who, "through the eternal Spirit offered himself to God",[1] and who now "ever lives to make intercession for us."[2] As for human beings, who falter in their attempts to pray, the Holy Spirit "helps us in our weakness; for we do not know how to pray as we ought, but that very Spirit intercedes for us with sighs too deep for words."[3] A well-known collect encapsulates this vision of prayer in the following words: "Blessed Lord, lifting up holy hands perpetually for all humankind, breathe by thy Holy Spirit such love into the prayers we offer, that they may be taken into thine, and prevail with thine, to the glory of thy holy name."[4]

If it is axiomatic that all prayer is gathered into the high-priestly prayer of Christ, it is no less so that all prayer is made in fellowship with Christ's body, the Church. The fourth chapter of the letter to the Ephesians paints a magnificent picture of individual Christians "growing up in every way into him who is the head, into Christ, from whom the whole body, joined and knitted together by every ligament with which it is equipped, as each part is working properly, promotes the body's growth in building itself up in love".[5] No Christian lives apart from the body of Christ, which unites him or her with Christ, and unites him or her with all other members of the body; and no Christian prays apart from Christ and Christ's body.

It does *not* follow from this that prayer can only be offered congregationally. The Lord himself prayed alone, and he taught his followers to seek out their "inner room" to pray to the Father "in secret".[6] At the same time, the Lord gave his disciples the Eucharist, which is necessarily corporate. It is supremely in the Eucharist that the body of Christ, implicit in every Christian prayer, is made explicit.

What of those who do not confess the faith of Christ but still pray to God? St Paul's frank admission that we do not know how to pray includes everyone: all people, whether or not they confess the faith of Christ, fall into the same category of prayerful ignorance and ignorant praying. In all longing hearts the Holy Spirit intercedes with sighs too deep for words; and we know from St John that the Spirit is not confined, but "blows where he wills".[7]

In considering the prayer that is offered in cathedrals, we need to bear these principles in mind. There is the corporate prayer of the Christian body, which we call the liturgy, the heart of which is the celebration of the sacraments and of the daily office. There is the less official but still corporate prayer offered on such occasions as school assemblies, carol services, memorial services, and all the other occasional acts of worship that make up so large a part of a cathedral's programme. There is the prayer of small groups, or individual Christians, or a day chaplain praying with a troubled visitor in a side chapel. There is the inarticulate prayer of the tourist who finds the lighting of a candle expressive of a longing "too deep for words". From a theological perspective, all this imperfect prayer is included in the perfect prayer of Christ, and is the action of the Church, Christ's body. From the particular perspective of a cathedral, this praying is varied, much of it unorganized, some of it unorthodox, but it is all part of the totality of the cathedral's offering of prayer.

THE CATHEDRAL AS THE BISHOP'S CHURCH

A cathedral church is defined by the *cathedra*, the chair which signifies the governing, teaching, and pastoring ministry of the bishop. In Anglican theology, the visible identity of the church is found in the reading of the holy scriptures, the confession of the catholic creeds, and the celebration of the sacraments of baptism and the Eucharist, served by the ministry of bishops in succession from "the apostles' time". When the bishop, from the chair of the cathedral church, presides at the liturgies of the word and of the sacraments, then the presence of the catholic Church in that place is expressed and embodied. At some times and in some parts of the Christian world this might be seen weekly or even daily, where it is or was the practice of the bishop to be the resident pastor of the cathedral. Such was the case in fourth-century Milan, when Augustine came to learn the faith from Bishop Ambrose. Such could still be found in rural Greece, when Peter Hammond published his celebrated account of the Greek church in 1956, *The Waters of Marah*.[8] But from the time of the expansion of the western church into northern Europe, dioceses have typically been too large for the bishop to pastor the flock in so intimate a way. The occasions today when the bishop presides at the liturgies of baptism or the Eucharist (typically Christmas, Easter, and Pentecost, the dedication or patronal feast of the cathedral, the chrism Eucharist in Holy Week, and the annual ordinations of deacons and priests, some at least of which may be listed in the cathedral statutes[9]) are therefore *special* occasions. All the same, occasional as they may be, there is still a sense in which these celebrations are *characteristic* of a cathedral. Here one glimpses, more than at other times, the people of the diocese gathered with their bishop in the cathedral church, to celebrate the central mysteries of the faith.

Some bishops build on this core of liturgical celebrations by a ministry of teaching conducted in the cathedral. Cardinal Martini (1927–2012), Archbishop of Milan from 1980 to 2002, packed his cathedral with a monthly *lectio divina* for young people; when the cathedral was full they spilled into other churches connected by CCTV. Other bishops may use their cathedrals for teaching mornings or quiet days. It is a powerful witness to tourists who arrive on a Saturday morning to find the nave silent but filled with Christians studying the scriptures under the leadership of the bishop. These too are moments when the cathedral expresses its fundamental role as the bishop's church.

THE MEDIAEVAL CATHEDRAL: MONASTIC AND COLLEGIATE FOUNDATIONS

Even in the times or places when the bishop was the resident pastor of the cathedral, he would be assisted by a "college" of priests, deacons, and other ministers. Where dioceses were large, and consequently the bishop's ministry more peripatetic, the body of assistant clergy naturally took on the role of the cathedral's permanent pastorate. In England, from the Anglo-Saxon period through to the twelfth century, three developments simultaneously distanced cathedrals from that patristic conception of a place where the bishop directly pastored the local church. The first was the increasing importance of bishops as great officers of state, drawing them away from their dioceses on the king's business. The second, almost unique to England, was the organization of some cathedrals as monastic communities, with the inevitable exclusion of any non-monastic local community. And the third, in those cathedrals which were served not by monks, but (like the cathedrals of continental Europe) by communities of "secular" priests, was the development of a distinct, quasi-monastic spirituality among the clergy, typified by celibacy, a common life, and a seven-fold daily office that was to all intents and purposes monastic.[10] By the end of the twelfth century, English cathedrals were *either* abbeys,[11] where the bishop held the title of abbot, but the day to day direction of the community was in the hands of the prior, *or* "collegiate" foundations comprising a chapter of residentiary canons, under the presidency of a dean. In both cases, the resident community of monks or canons occupied the screened-off quire for the daily high mass and offices. The layfolk were restricted to attending mass at a "parish altar" in the nave, or at one of the side altars, or in the parish churches of the town.

The bishop, too, was side-lined. The *cathedra* was usually no more than a stall on the south side of the quire, either at the east or the west end, the grandeur of which could not disguise the fact that this was not a place from which he could preside at the Eucharist or teach the people.[12]

This phase of English cathedral life lasted until the Reformation, but has left its profound mark on cathedral life to this day. It is a vision of the cathedral community as a resident clerical foundation (whether of monks or canons) whose task it was to offer the praises of God daily. It mattered not if neither the bishop nor the laity was present or absent. The raison d'être of the cathedral life was no longer to be the place of the bishop's ministry of governing, teaching, and pastoring the diocese, which for the most part the bishop now did elsewhere. Nor was it to be the spiritual home of a local congregation of lay people, with baptisms or marriages and the care of the sick and dying. The task of the resident body of the cathedral was praise and prayer, offered day in and day out, in the Eucharist and the divine office. Of course, from a mediaeval perspective, that offering of prayer made a vital contribution to the wellbeing of society. Alongside the knights who fought and the peasants who laboured were the monks and clerks who prayed. So to the mediaeval mind, cathedrals were not withdrawn from the world, even though the increasingly elaborate round of the Eucharist and the office were practically exclusive: they bore up the pillars of the earth.

THE POST-REFORMATION CATHEDRAL

The effect of the Reformation on English cathedrals was profound in some ways, but not in others. No cathedral was closed down. In all cases the administrative, financial, and commercial operation of the cathedrals, now the owners of vast estates, found a way to carry on. The monasteries were dissolved, but the constitution of the old "secular" cathedrals was imposed on the monastic cathedrals, often with a large measure of continuity. At Worcester, for instance, the last prior became the first dean, and the twelve new canons were monks from the former cathedral priory. The statutes of King Henry VIII make it clear that the dean and chapter were to continue to celebrate the seven-fold divine office (still, of course, in Latin); the night office was the only one to be discontinued. Similar arrangements were made at other formerly monastic cathedrals. Some of the great abbey churches were preserved and given cathedral status, with deans and canons.[13]

The post-Reformation English cathedral thus emerged organically from mediaeval practice, with much of the mediaeval spirituality clinging to it. Even when the liturgy was put into English, and the seven-fold office reduced to the two offices of mattins and evensong, there was still the expectation that these resident clerical communities would offer the daily praise of the church, and that neither the presence of the bishop nor of a local lay congregation was necessary to that activity. The resident community, sometimes known as the "college" or the "foundation", consisted of the dean and canons, minor canons, lay clerks, choristers, and schoolmasters. There was an expectation in the early statutes that this body would pray together daily, study together daily, and in some places eat together daily. But the clergy could now marry, so private households also appeared in the close. Wives, children, and domestic staff made up a little lay "parish", but their presence only reinforced the impression that a cathedral was predominantly an exclusive clerical community.

It is not too much to say that, the dissolution of the monasteries notwithstanding, a certain Benedictine ethos survived and flourished. The cathedral close with its comfortable residences, the butt of so much humour and hostility, could still at its best be a place of both hospitality and learning. Today, cathedrals which once were Benedictine foundations now value that history, and speak of their "Benedictine" heritage and vocation. Local monastic communities often collaborate with cathedrals in their ministry to visitors or their teaching programme, and in some cases the relationship is expressed in the cathedral statutes.[14] It has, indeed, been remarked that Anglicanism as a whole bears a certain Benedictine stamp.[15]

The vision of a cathedral as a "foundation" devoted to prayer survives today. It is the justification for the effort and expense of maintaining a musical establishment capable of the best liturgical music, singing evensong daily even though the musicians and clergy may outnumber the rest of the worshippers. It is the justification for the daily celebration of the Eucharist on 365 days of the year, on some of which days only the celebrant and the verger may be present. In this vision of what a cathedral is, the overriding obligation is the daily worship of almighty God, day by day. Congregational statistics, which so bedevil other areas of church life today, are irrelevant to this conception of a cathedral. And even if the mediaeval idea that society was sustained by those who fought, laboured, or prayed, has vanished, there is a residual sense that it is the task of the Church of England and its clergy to pray for the nation, and in most cathedral cities that sense is very definitely embodied in the cathedral.

THE CATHEDRAL COMMUNITY

Cathedral foundations remained predominantly clerical throughout the nineteenth century, but the end of that century saw the laity beginning to return. They returned in the form of tourists, as tourism grew. They returned as late Victorian chapters initiated programmes of restoration, abolished admission charges, and introduced "congregational" services (typically a second evensong with a sermon on a Sunday, sung by a voluntary choir, and held in the nave). In the early twentieth century, laypeople were encouraged to join organized "Friends" of cathedrals, in which they could hold office, and perhaps even express opinions about how their cathedral was run. Later on in the same century, restoration "trusts" were formed in many places, and here laypeople might hold real power, administering large sums of money and expecting a proper negotiation with the chapter about its expenditure. At the same time the popularity of, first, the bicycle and then the car gave a new freedom to church-going (as well as a new freedom for using Sundays for other purposes as well). People, if they went to church at all, could now choose where they went; and quite a few found that they liked attending cathedrals as their "parish church". The regular Sunday morning cathedral congregation was born.

By now some old parish churches had become cathedrals without losing their parochial status. Where new dioceses were created, to match the new cities and large centres of population, only three new cathedrals were built (Truro, Liverpool, Guildford). In other cases, large parish churches were adapted or enlarged, and in most cases a type of cathedral constitution, governed by a provost and chapter, was bolted on to a parochial organization of churchwardens and (later) parochial church councillors. Until the office of provost was abolished in the Cathedrals Measure of 1999, "parish-church cathedrals" could be clearly distinguished from dean-and-chapter cathedrals. But the reality was that all cathedrals had acquired something of a parochial character.

Throughout the middle years of the twentieth century, the Church of England became more eucharistic. The celebration of the Eucharist (whether called "parish communion", "sung Eucharist", or "high mass") replaced sung mattins in many parishes as the principal service of the day (as the *Book of Common Prayer* had always envisaged). It was a natural evolution of cathedral life, then, to introduce a choral celebration of the Eucharist before, after, or instead of choral mattins, and that is now the norm in virtually every English cathedral today, attended by a substantial congregation of both regular worshippers and visitors, and often accompanied by such features of "parish" life as lay readers, intercessors, and eucharistic ministers, and a Sunday school. And when the bishop comes to preside at the Eucharist on the great feasts of the year, it feels less of an incursion into normal cathedral life and more of a natural taking of the bishop's place in the heart of the cathedral community.

There is an irony here. As Anglican parish life today becomes more fragile and less eucharistic, the principal Sunday Eucharist may seem more typically "cathedral" than "parochial". Yet the revival of the cathedral Eucharist owes its place to the revival of the Eucharist in the parish, which in turn was obedient to that vision of the centrality of the Eucharist which the Prayer Book inherited from the patristic and mediaeval church. What has now been added is a substantial congregation of laypeople at the main cathedral Eucharist each Sunday, which had scarcely been seen in England for a thousand years.

It would be a mistake, however, to see the "parochial" character of modern cathedrals simply in terms of "regular" worshippers. Parish churches and cathedrals welcome occasional worshippers, both to their regular weekly services and to services on special occasions, and the latter (such as Christmas carol services) may attract the largest numbers of any service in the year. Indeed, at least some of the current reputation of cathedrals to be places of numerical "growth" reflects attendance at such occasional services.[16]

THE CATHEDRAL AS SHRINE

The emergence of what the Cathedrals Measure 1999 calls "the cathedral community" has substantially modified, but not replaced, the older conception of the cathedral as a clerical "college" or "foundation". As we have just seen, the "community" model in some ways sits more easily with the still older "episcopal/diocesan" model than with the clerical foundation (in which much energy was expended, in practice, in keeping the bishop at arm's length). But before we examine more deeply the different kinds of praying engendered by these different conceptions of what a cathedral is, there are two more levels of church life to consider. The first of these is what we might call, the cathedral as a "shrine church".

When, in Trollope's novel *The Warden*, Mr Harding paid his twopence to enter Westminster Abbey "as a sightseer" because it was not yet open for the morning service,[17] there was a very clear distinction between tourists and worshippers. Those cathedrals which find themselves once more having to charge for entry struggle to overcome that unwelcome distinction. Who has worked in a cathedral and cannot tell stories of people entering "as a sightseer" and then encountering the presence of God? Even Philip Larkin felt compelled to take off his cycle clips "in awkward reverence" when he visited a country church and recognized it as "a serious house on serious earth".[18]

We can see that what became known in the early nineteenth century as "tourism" was the secularizing of a natural yearning to travel, which in more pious centuries took the form of pilgrimage. The holy places of Jerusalem, made accessible by St Helena after the Peace of the Church, attracted the pilgrim Egeria in the fourth century, and from that time on, restless Christians combined piety with adventure by journeying to Jerusalem or Rome or Compostela. Without leaving England, pilgrims could travel to the shrine of Our Lady of Walsingham, or St Edward the

Confessor at Westminster, or the "holy blissful martyr" St Thomas of Canterbury. Every mediaeval diocese notched up its tally of shrines, and by the end of the Middle Ages there could have been few people who were not more than a couple of days' walking from the shrine of a saint. Cathedrals excelled in the spiritual attractions offered to the energetic pilgrim, with a Lady Chapel, the tomb of a local saint or two, and an impressive store of relics, annually displayed on "the feast of the relics" each October.

The presence of an important shrine might lead to the substantial remodelling of the building. The rebuilding of the Norman cathedral at Worcester in the Gothic style in the reign of Henry III was prompted by the desire to "translate" the shrines of St Oswald and St Wulfstan, and to construct a new chapel of Our Lady, as well as to do honour to the burial place of the less-than-saintly King John. At Chichester, the irregular cloister appears to be a covered walkway to enable pilgrims to enter and leave the cathedral at the most convenient points to visit the three shrines connected to St Richard.[19] The floor of the nave at Chartres slopes towards the west door, to facilitate the washing out of the cathedral made necessary by the large number of pilgrims who slept there. If we can project our imaginations back to the later Middle Ages, we may suppose that the monks or canons sometimes struggled to keep the liturgical round going amid the press of jostling pilgrims. Modern cathedral chapters, balancing the pressures of tourism and the requirements of worship, know how they felt.

The point, however, is that modern visitors, whether they see themselves as pilgrims or tourists, are treading in the footsteps of those who very definitely came as pilgrims; so a modern cathedral chapter, as guardians of an ancient shrine, will seek to give them some glimpse of the holy, some sense of it being a "serious house". Hence the racks of prayer cards, prayer trees, intercession boards, the side chapel set aside (not always successfully) for "private" prayer, the call to prayer over the sound-system every hour, and the lighting of votive candles. Like the mediaeval pilgrims, modern visitors will sometimes attend a service, either because they meant to, or because they decided on the spur of the moment to do so. (It is to be hoped that all cathedral staff today expect and welcome this, and no visitor will be stopped as the author, when a teenager, was stopped by a stentorian voice: "You can't go in there—there's going to be a *service!*")

A GLOBAL CONGREGATION

The final form of church life that we should consider is the cathedral as a "virtual" church. For the past ninety years, BBC Radio 3 has broadcast Choral Evensong. The first great television spectacle in this country was the Coronation, embedded in a celebration of the Holy Communion according to the *Book of Common Prayer*. From those days on, and more than ever in the era of social media, cathedral chapters know that they have a ministry and a congregation which are potentially global. Those who have had the experience of a Christmas Day television broadcast, or an Easter Day radio broadcast, know that Boxing Day or Easter Monday may be spent reading emails from viewers in the Hebrides, or defending the sermon to a listener in the Scillies. A sermon published on the cathedral website may console someone in Australia or enrage someone in America. And the postcard which comes from the person housebound or in hospital who says that we "made" their Christmas or their Easter, and that they pray for us in return, leaves us in no doubt that these people too are part of our congregation and contribute to the praying life of cathedrals.

"TEACH US TO PRAY"

We began with the axiom that all human prayer is an imperfect participating in the perfect prayer of Christ the eternal high priest, and from St Paul's confession that "we do not know how to pray as we ought." Alongside that confession, however, must be set the request of the disciples, "Lord, teach us to pray, as John taught his disciples."[20] The praying Christian longs to pray better; longs, as Paul also said, to be changed from one degree of glory to another by the transforming glory of God reflected in the face of Jesus Christ.[21] Christ's response to the disciples' request was to give them the "Our Father": a simple but fundamental piece of *liturgical formation*. Implicit in that exchange between Christ and his disciples is the obligation of the church not only to provide a space where prayer can be offered, but also to be a community where prayer is taught.

Cathedrals offer great opportunities for the teaching of prayer, but the sheer diversity of cathedral life can be an obstacle. If it is the case that there are at least six ecclesial identities embodied in a modern cathedral, it is not the case that people conveniently divide themselves into six different categories of worshipper. The great diocesan occasion, presided over by the bishop, may be attended by many people with little connection with the church, especially if they are the friends and relations of those being ordained, confirmed, or baptized. Choral Evensong may be attended by some, or many, who are ill-prepared to engage with its high scriptural content.[22] The Sunday Eucharist in many cathedrals, especially in the summer months, will have a significant number of casual visitors, some of them waiting for the cathedral to re-open for "visiting". It is often remarked that cathedrals are places where people can hover on the margins without being pressured into a participation for which they are unready. Perhaps the question must also be asked as to what cathedrals do to encourage that greater participation, and in particular, what are the modes of liturgical formation which a cathedral offers to those who might wish to participate more intelligently?

In spite of the obstacles, the opportunities are great. Tailor-made orders of service can convey crisp and imaginative liturgical explanation. Advent and Lent courses are good for deepening awareness of the liturgy of the seasons. Leaflets in a chapel set aside for quiet prayer can prompt the casual visitor to prayerful reflection, as can audio-tours and mobile phone apps. Notices at a candle-stand invite passers-by to reflect on their hopes and fears, and make a prayer of them. Punctuating the day with an hourly announcement over the sound-system may be the first experience a visitor has ever had of being invited to contribute to the prayer of the church. And every sermon, school assembly address, introduction to an act of worship, greeting to a group of visitors, or welcome to a concert can, if sensitively done, be an implicit invitation to prayer or, at the very least, an indication that here is a "serious house on serious earth".

CONCLUSION

We have identified at least six ecclesial identities present in a modern English cathedral: (1) the cathedral as the bishop's church, surviving from the age of the Fathers, the era when cathedrals were invented; (2) the cathedral as a monastery, uniquely flourishing in England until the dissolution, but with a contemporary legacy of "ethos"; (3) the cathedral as a "college" or "foundation", a small and predominantly clerical/choral community, focused on the daily office; (4) the cathedral as parish or quasi-parish church, with a regular lay congregation, and a "fringe" of occasional services; (5) the cathedral as a shrine, a resort for visitors, whether considered as pilgrims or tourists; and (6) the cathedral as a virtual church, addressing a global congregation. Each identity is a palimpsest, superimposed on the previous ones, modifying them but not effacing them.

A cathedral may shift through all six ecclesial identities in the course of a single day, but if each is a manifestation of the catholic Church in that particular place uniting those who pray with the communion of saints, this suggests that no *one* ecclesial identity may claim precedence. The cathedral church as bishop's church may have a constitutional and historical priority; the cathedral as a "foundation" may reflect most closely the day-to-day autonomy of an English cathedral; the cathedral as an actual or quasi parish church may be the most important thing to the many laypeople who now make their cathedral their spiritual home; but to claim that any one of these had an objective priority of status would be to overlook the point at which we began. Each prayer offered in a cathedral, whether embodied in the last exquisite note of Choral Evensong hanging in the air, or in the inarticulate sigh of the visitor in distress who lights a candle, is a part of Christ's prayer and a part of the church's prayer. It is not the preserve of an ecclesiastical elite, be that episcopal, capitular, or congregational. The prayer which is offered in cathedrals, as elsewhere, is the prayer of those who do not know how to pray, even if they long to do so; and it is the *Lord* of the church, and not the church, who takes that prayer and makes it perfect.[23]

NOTES

1. Hebrews 9. 14.
2. Hebrews 7. 25.
3. Romans 8. 26.
4. Eric Milner-White (ed.), *After the Third Collect: Prayers and Thanksgivings for Use in Public Worship* (A.R. Mowbray & Co. Ltd, 1938), p. 83; from *A Cambridge Bede Book* (Longmans, 1936).
5. Ephesians 4. 15–16.
6. Luke 11. 1; Matthew 6. 1–6.
7. John 3. 8.
8. "For all the dignity attaching to his high office the Greek bishop is commonly the most approachable of men; the sheer accessibility of the generality of bishops of the country dioceses is a matter for wonder and rejoicing in a world fallen beneath the curse of an impersonal and irresponsible bureaucracy. Every morning, his liturgy fulfilled, the metropolitan takes his seat in his office and all the world comes to see him . . . (he) sits at his desk beneath an eikon of the Pantokrator, questioning, counselling, reproving and writing letters of commendation, while a stalwart archimandrite leans against the door with outstretched arm to keep the multitude without at bay." Peter Hammond, *The Waters of Marah: The Present State of the Greek Church* (Rockcliff, 1956), p. 34. The form for the confirmation of the election of a diocesan bishop in the Church of England still refers to the "bishop and pastor of the cathedral church of *x*", a remarkable survival of a patristic conception of a bishop's ministry.
9. At Worcester, for instance, the diocesan bishop presides as of right on the Feast of St Wulfstan; at Chichester, on the Feast of St Richard.
10. The origins of colleges or chapters of "secular" (i.e. non-monastic) priests did indeed lie far back in the patristic period. St Augustine established such a community as his household at Hippo, and the "rule of St Augustine" was later adopted by many religious houses in western Europe.
11. All of them Benedictine, apart from Carlisle, which was an abbey of Augustinian Regular Canons from the foundation of the See of Carlisle in 1133 until its dissolution in 1540. Bristol was also an abbey of Augustinian Regular Canons from its foundation in 1140 to its dissolution, after which it was made the cathedral church of the new diocese of Bristol in 1542.

12. The ancient (Saxon?) *cathedra* remains in the ancient presidential position in the Romanesque apse at Norwich. The thirteenth-century "chair of St Augustine" at Canterbury has in recent years been given a central place.

13. Bristol, Chester, Gloucester, Oxford, Peterborough, and, for a few years only, Westminster. Henry VIII's original plan was for a larger number.

14. At Worcester, in addition to two "ecumenical canons", the statutes provide for the heads of the two Anglican communities in the diocese, Mucknell Abbey (Benedictine) and Glasshampton Monastery (Franciscan), and for the monk of the English Benedictine Congregation who holds the titular office of "Prior of Worcester", to be made honorary canons.

15. See, for instance, Robert Hale, *Canterbury and Rome: Sister Churches* (Darton, Longman and Todd, 1982).

16. On cathedral carol services and who attends them, and why, see the essay by David S. Walker, Bishop of Manchester, in Leslie J. Francis (ed.), *Anglican Cathedrals in Modern Life: The Science of Cathedral Studies* (Palgrave Macmillan, 2015), pp. 111–130.

17. Anthony Trollope, *The Warden*, first published 1855, chapter xvi.

18. Philip Larkin, "Church Going" in *Collected Poems* (Marvell Press and Faber & Faber, 1988), pp. 97–98.

19. His original place of burial in the Chapel of St Thomas and St Edmund; his shrine in the retroquire; his head separately displayed in the Chapel of St Mary Magdalen.

20. Luke 11. 1.

21. Cf. 2 Corinthians 3. 18; 4. 6.

22. The Additional Weekday Lectionary was designed to soften the impact of undigested and unexplained scripture readings at evensong (<https://www.churchofengland.org/media/1172737/2010%20additional%20weekday%20lectionary.pdf>).

23. Readers of this volume may be interested in Michael Brierley (ed.), *Life After Tragedy: Essays on Faith and the First World War Evoked by Geoffrey Studdert Kennedy* (Cascade Books, 2017). Most of these essays are by authors from within Worcester Diocese where Studdert Kennedy was a priest. Michael Brierley is the Precentor of Worcester Cathedral.

9.   FOCUSES OF PROPHECY?

Nicholas Henshall

INTRODUCTION

Cathedrals stand in a creatively marginal place in relationship both to the institutional structures of the Church and to the wider networks of society. This—if recognized and developed appropriately—gives cathedrals a unique and powerful prophetic voice. This unusual context is unique to the cathedrals of the Church of England. It is an ambiguity well caught by much of the symbolic language of cathedrals: it is the bishop's church, and yet the bishop knocks on the door to gain entry. Cathedrals are distinctively the seat of the bishop and centres of Christian worship and mission,[1] but they also very clearly function as neutral convening space, as public spaces for all. From the launch of the Range Rover Evoque in Liverpool Cathedral to an Imam singing from the Quran at a Holocaust Memorial Day event in Derby Cathedral, these buildings deliver much of their mission through the strength of the networks they hold. This enables them to speak powerfully in the public square and to the Church.

The creatively marginal space occupied by cathedrals sometimes appears to be better understood by secular networks than by church structures. It gives cathedrals significant freedom both to speak and to act—whether in areas of contemporary moral debate or in the delivery of radically transformative social programmes. It is not that cathedrals stand in a place of privilege and power. That might be true of only a small number of "old foundation" and "new foundation" cathedrals. In reality the largest grouping of English cathedrals is those founded since 1836, almost all of which combine parochial obligations with cathedral identity.[2] Of course, all cathedrals have learnt that making assumptions about their own importance and their right to be there is the surest way to lose the networks that constitute the cathedral's mission field in city, diocese, and region.

Let me define my terms. By "focus" I do not mean that certain activities are the prerogative of the cathedrals, but that a cathedral exemplifies, through these activities, something critically important about the nature of the Church and the Christian gospel for the networks of diocese, city, and region—i.e. the Church and the public square. This is precisely because it is "the bishop's church and a centre of worship and mission". Many—even most—of these activities are engaged in by all sorts of other churches, but they are activities in which the cathedral as the bishop's church *must* or *should* engage. So, for example, the particular international ministry of reconciliation based at Coventry Cathedral is a ministry of the whole church, characteristic of a cathedral. It could be based in another context, but that would be limiting rather than liberating. Then, defining my terms further, by "prophecy" I mean both telling and acting out gospel values and the nature of Christian discipleship in general, again specifically as the bishop's church. This points the Church and the networks of the wider community to what Christian faith looks like. Part of this is the complex and controversial role of the cathedrals' critique of church institutions.

CATHEDRALS—A CONTEMPORARY ANOMALY

"The seat of the bishop and a centre of worship and mission" is a minimal definition of what a cathedral is or should be. It has little virtue beyond its brevity. But in trying to work out what that looks like in practice, cathedrals have, in the first place, developed a range of more or less adequate "straplines", and secondly, backed these up with proper strategic planning. Most cathedrals would doubtless wish that they had thought of Liverpool Cathedral's strapline—"A safe place to do risky things in Christ's service"—but Justin Welby just got there first!

At the heart of this (and other straplines) is the conviction that there is something unique about English cathedrals arising out of that minimal description (the seat of the bishop and a centre of worship and mission). This uniqueness gives cathedrals a special place in the life of the nation. In the late decades of the twentieth century, cathedrals had been growing through bold experiment and through significant changes in governance and accountability.[3] So the 1990s saw the completion of Portsmouth Cathedral and other challenging work there, saw the Archer Project at Sheffield Cathedral, feeding homeless and other needy people, saw the completion of the education centre at Canterbury, saw the largest additional cathedral buildings since the Reformation built at Norwich, and, of course, saw the remarkable developments at both Southwark and Bury St Edmunds, with completion of its tower and transepts—the final emergence of the "cathedral for Suffolk". Cathedrals of all kinds have engaged in innovative thinking and challenging work.

BUT HOW ARE CATHEDRALS UNIQUE?

The question arises partly because of the attention given in recent years to the fact that cathedral congregations have been growing since the millennium. Certainly most cathedrals had realized by the early years of this new millennium that something was going on. In some cathedrals there was a growth in Sunday attendance; in most, growth in weekday attendance; and in all, growth in attendance at festivals. This is what powered both the secular headlines and the attention of the wider church when the report "From Anecdote to Evidence" was published in 2014,[4] claiming 34 per cent growth in cathedral attendances over a ten-year period. The Dean of Wells, John Davies—at that time Dean of Derby—raised the pertinent question of whether it was the job of cathedrals to grow. The overwhelmingly interesting thing may not be that cathedrals are growing, but that this growth appears to be unique to English cathedrals. Therefore the most interesting question of all is, in what sense are they unique?

Here I want to suggest that their uniqueness lies in both their role as a focus of prophecy and their scope precisely as "the seat of the bishop and a centre of worship and mission". "Seat of the bishop" means that the cathedral is a mission centre or resource for the whole region and has an active ministry across the diocese. The very nature of English cathedrals means that the active ingredient they bring to the table is precisely that they embody a parallel spiritual and emotional (rather than juridical) set of understandings about the mission and ministry of the Church which are in critical dialogue with the Church and wider networks. This critical dialogue has real dangers—cathedrals have sometimes been thorns in the side of the dioceses they are there to serve; at other times they have simply been irrelevant. And the ambivalence and ambiguity sometimes historically present in the relationships between bishop and dean has not been unknown in more recent periods—sometimes, but not always, to the detriment of both. Cathedrals have a certain independence, but they must use it wisely. It is certainly a big claim that cathedrals represent a complementary stream of spiritual and emotional authority, rather than juridical control, but it is not meant to be oppositional or antagonistic. It is the case that some critics suggest cathedrals are still functioning in Christendom mode; cathedrals, however, have increasingly been able to demonstrate that they are in the forefront of renegotiating the contract between church and society, in an energetic recognition both that this relationship had changed forever by the late 1990s and that this was a genuine opportunity rather than a disaster. As the following decade was to show, cathedrals were able to deliver renewal and reform.

It is worth noting that in Brown and Woodhead's provocative and critical book *That Was The Church That Was*[5] cathedrals are barely mentioned. That is partly because cathedrals simply do not fit the thesis or narrative of the book. Indeed, Brown and Woodhead recognize this: ". . . they have been unexpectedly successful in rejuvenating themselves in the last few decades." (p. 97). Cathedrals are growing and evolving, and are deeply engaged in and serving their context and culture. Above all, perhaps, as one cathedral administrator new to cathedrals said on starting work, "Cathedrals simply are not that churchy"—by which she meant something profoundly positive in contrast to her previous experience of the Church. The cathedral felt explicitly like a thriving, outward-facing community. Although deans sit on the Bishop's Staff Meeting, and some *become* bishops, cathedrals lie almost entirely outside the synodical and hierarchical structures and cultures that Brown and Woodhead take to be the Church of England. Potentially this is hugely positive for the wider church, as cathedrals—like the new monastic communities in France[6]— may well become reservoirs for renewal.

There is, in part, a complex dialogue between bishops and cathedrals, and indeed between national church and cathedrals, because they inhabit different and distinctive narratives. At the most basic level, bishops have often been handling a narrative of decline while cathedrals are handling a narrative of growth and development. The invitation here is to make these narratives complementary and to recognize that the cathedral can provide critical distance and help build capacity in and for the diocese.

MISSION AND SCOPE

The way cathedrals are resourced and governed may be unusual, but it sends a huge message to all stakeholders in the life of the cathedral (of which the congregations—however significant—are only one). Cathedrals are resourced essentially as the national church's free gift to the diocese. Certainly there may emerge changes to cathedral funding, but the principle is important: each cathedral receives from the Church Commissioners a dean and two canons—not to run a big church for either a local or an eclectic community, but rather to run a cathedral for a diocese, and hence for the secular city and regional networks too. It is for this reason that deans and canons are often "out and about" across the diocese leading worship, preaching, speaking at a study weekend, taking a quiet day— because (again, uniquely to English cathedrals) the dean is the dean of the *city*, not the *cathedral*. This is not about status (which is rarely recognized anyway) but about service: the dean, as senior priest in the diocese, shares in the bishop's ministry as teacher and evangelist to the whole diocese. Cathedral congregations frequently find this very puzzling, especially in cathedrals where their primary historic identity has been as a big parish church. It is certainly, for some, a challenging lesson to learn that the chapter is not there primarily to serve the Sunday congregations but to take forward the mission and ministry of the cathedral across the networks of the city, the diocese, and the region.

Cathedral governance tells the same story. The core governing body, the chapter, is not constructed as a church council but as a small number of lay trustees alongside the dean and canons. Even in cathedrals with roots as parish churches, the chapter has minimal representation from the congregation. The cathedral is not so much there to speak for itself but is fundamentally an outward-facing community using its resources not inwardly, to keep the show on the road, but outwardly, in service of the complex overlapping networks through which it delivers its mission. Many parishes and local Christian communities do not see this core aspect of the cathedral's mission and ministry with any clarity, and many cathedrals have a history of distance from the life of the diocese. Cathedrals are addressing this—deans and canons are available for Sunday duty across the diocese, not just in glamorous, high-profile places; they lead deanery events, even inviting themselves to speak at deanery synods—seeking to explain again what a cathedral is and how it can be good news for a diocese, an active ingredient in the mission and ministry of the Church more widely. It is a lengthy task because it is about building and sustaining relationships. Building these relationships helps structurally. Two cathedrals so far have taken the bold step of making all area deans (and in one case all deanery lay chairs) honorary canons. Although challenging, it moves the College of Canons along to become a genuinely strategic group within the diocese. Again and again cathedrals need to demonstrate that they are genuinely outward-facing, at the service of the networks of city, diocese, and region. One new dean discovered, on arrival, that the chaplain to the County Council offices next door to the cathedral was a vicar from elsewhere. She was doing a good job, but the dean knew that it was a terrible indictment of the cathedral's ministry, a sign of just how far it had lost its way, that the cathedral had somehow lost this key outward-facing ministry.

Cathedrals learn in different ways, certainly, and history and context determine much about what they feel they can take for granted. I grew up in east Manchester, in the Diocese of Chester, but there was no doubt that Chester was "our" cathedral, even though you had to travel through a whole different diocese to get there. In Liverpool, nowhere in the diocese is further than twenty-seven miles from the cathedral. The building itself is non-negotiable. Many smaller urban cathedrals seeking to serve much larger dioceses constantly need to earn their right to be there if they are to build the relationships across the diocese through which they will fulfil their mission. The late Michael Perham, when Dean of Derby, knew that ministry to the city and the diocese was the lifeblood of the cathedral's mission: a cathedral such as Derby (and the same is certainly true at Chelmsford) could assume no historic privileges and must earn the right to sit at anyone else's table. But precisely in doing that—working with the inter-faith networks; being recognized as a credible partner by the City Council; working closely with the local media; being prepared to drive a 90-mile round trip on a dark winter evening to lead a deanery synod's strategic planning session—all of these are not add-ons to the cathedral's ministry but models of its prophetic focus, and thus active ingredients. It works both ways. A cathedral quite naturally provides a focus for diocesan and regional events—ordinations, farmers' harvests, Remembrance Day. But chapters are wise enough not to take these opportunities for granted and are prepared to do the legwork.

The following may not be a model for everywhere, but is offered here as an example. At my installation as Dean I preached on the word "Mass". It is the word Roman Catholics, and indeed also Scandinavian Lutherans, use for the Eucharist, and the word I had grown up with. Although it will conjure up a range of responses, the word simply means, "Get out of here!" Having met my new colleagues and understood something of the life of the cathedral, its relation to the public square, and its place in the diocese, a theme around "being sent" emerged. What did it mean for a cathedral to be an apostolic community, a "sent" community? This has since become central to our self-understanding as a cathedral, and indeed to our strategic plan.

In our diocese's centenary year, the bishop challenged every church community to have some form of mission event. The response was enthusiastic, resulting in a wide range of imaginative pieces of outreach. But what would a cathedral mission event look like? Each Thursday

morning the ministry team here meets to do *lectio divina* and to reflect—
not to act as a governance group or an executive group; this is not a time
for decisions. It is the place from which all the best things that have
happened here have come. One Thursday we were drawn to the realization
that, for our mission event, we would cancel the main services at the
cathedral and send everyone elsewhere. There were complaints, outrage,
incomprehension. But in the end hundreds of people went out to parishes
and communities across the diocese, and then came back to share their
stories—of worship and welcome, of tiny congregations who needed
support, of great charismatic churches which had something important
to say to the cathedral, of a tiny Baptist church which apparently "felt just
like the cathedral". That day—and there has been an annual repeat ever
since, now with no anger or dissension—literally turned the cathedral
inside out. It had an impact on our relationship of service with a very
wide range of churches and communities. It began to move forward the
cathedral's own self-understanding—not as a big building in Chelmsford
that was home to thriving congregations, but as a mission resource and a
network for the churches and communities of the diocese.

BRAND

Cathedral as *brand* certainly appears to play well in the "secular" networks.
When the new John Lewis store opened in a big city centre, they naturally
invited the cathedral choir to sing at the opening. In a different city, the
new Premier Inn immediately used a picture of the local cathedral on
all their branding. Ancient cathedrals are used to this kind of brand
recognition, but it is clearly now the case for many small modern cathedrals
too—indeed, young cities show a real pride in their "new" cathedrals. As
cathedral deans are also the senior priests in their diocese—therefore
sharing in and supporting the bishop's ministry, of whose seat they are
guardian—they are also deans of the place and context which is iconic
for city and region. Again, there is huge variety across cathedrals, mostly
determined by context, but chapters and cathedrals have an open invitation

to exercise a special role of civic leadership in local networks. This is a complex and challenging role to earn in the first place (and in most places it has to be earned) and a complex and challenging role to exercise, but the dean may become a critical friend to the Leader of the City Council, the Chief Constable, the local MP.

Once more, this demands time and work from the cathedral and its staff. Chapters must include people whose first response is to say "Yes". In one small city, following a cathedral service celebrating twenty-five years of town twinning, with representatives of the twin towns present, a German mayor challenged the dean to make the return trip six weeks later to preach at their town's great pre-Christmas gathering on Advent Sunday. The outcome of the dean saying "Yes" was a positive reappraisal of the cathedral as civic space, and genuine delight that the cathedral wanted to be a key partner in a major civic project. This is just one small example, but that the cathedral is sufficiently present alongside the civic and regional networks is not a matter of chance.

Best of all in my personal experience, on my arrival at the cathedral in Chelmsford, was the new Vice Chancellor of the local university coming to see me to ask if the graduations could be held at the cathedral. It was what we had literally been praying for. When I asked the Vice Chancellor why, he simply said, "Because the cathedral is *the* civic space at the heart of the city." This notion of civic space, public space, cultural space, space for all, is virtually unique to the cathedral and a powerful part of the cathedral's prophetic ministry. "Speaking truth to power" is far too glib a phrase for this. It is the cathedral's role as enabler, credible partner, bearer of a different set of values that enables it to make a unique contribution. I happened to be having a formal meeting with the Leader of Chelmsford City Council just as he had received a diagnosis of life-threatening cancer. Of course we prayed together and—as I always carry oils—I anointed him. It was not a remarkable piece of ministry but instead simply what a priest does. We have to be there to do it—not just showing up, but earning our right to access.

CATHEDRALS AS THE PLACE OF FORMATION

Cathedrals have a core role as the place of formation in the diocese. The comments by Stephen Cottrell at the end of this chapter will suggest just that. It is important to recognize that formation of all sorts takes place across Christian communities, and in formal terms through colleges and courses. But it is somehow key to the identity of the cathedral *for* the diocese. This too is prophetic, related to the cathedral's identity not as a source of authority in competition with the authority of the bishop and with the training provision of the diocese, but as part of the cathedral's role as liberated space. In this sense, it stands outside but complementary to diocesan structures—what I have referred to above as a parallel spiritual and emotional (rather than juridical) set of understandings about mission and ministry. That it is natural for the bishop's church, the place of ordination, to be also the place where vocations to all sorts of ministry are both nurtured and supported is not too big a claim. This is not primarily about practicalities and resources, although it is clear that many—even most—cathedrals have space and expertise to provide precisely this. Primarily it is about the cathedral's fundamental nature and call. This is well illustrated by the development of St Mellitus College, founded in 2007 and growing, in part, out of Holy Trinity, Brompton. St Mellitus is now one of the largest providers of theological formation in the Church of England, with some 650 students over three centres. As it has expanded so far, cathedrals have been key partners—first, Chelmsford Cathedral and, more recently, Liverpool, with the cathedral deans becoming members of the college staff. Chelmsford is also the first cathedral in the country to host a three-year mixed mode student from St Mellitus, London, on a three-year internship, as well as a three-year student from the Centre for Youth Ministry at Ridley Hall.

This is significant—seeing cathedrals as the natural place of formation. As new patterns of priestly formation emerge, cathedrals need to position themselves as willing partners in a ministry that both works with the grain of their identity and widens their scope. It is deeply moving to see students from widely differing backgrounds worshipping, praying, and studying together in their cathedral, beginning to encounter the cathedral as a community and a network rather than just a building or resource. They are also exposed to the formative patterns of daily prayer and praise that underpin the cathedral's life. This spills over into the cathedral's wider ministry—it becomes a place for clergy quiet days, resilience days, training days, well-being days, study days. Again, this is not simply (or even primarily) because of the cathedral's resources, but because of what it is for the diocese. The Baptist church around the corner has far superior audio-visual equipment, but the cathedral is still the right context for such work.

CATHEDRALS AND SOCIAL OUTREACH PROGRAMMES

A bishop preparing to lead a Cathedral Visitation (a kind of Ofsted inspection for cathedrals) said, "And I'll want to know what they're doing about the poor!" This sounds very paternalist, certainly, but it is a powerful question, and a necessary corollary to the cathedral's prophetic role in the public square. Like every aspect of the cathedral's life, it cuts both ways: it is about the direct delivery of ministry to the vulnerable and it is about the cathedral as the bishop's church. This makes this kind of service emblematic and exemplary, and thoroughly evangelical. Certainly cathedrals need to be humble about their offering. There are parish churches which are able to deliver far more in terms of social transformation programmes than most cathedrals, but that is to miss the point. Yes, all churches should be delivering social programmes for the poor in their context (and not just paying other people to do them). This is an absolutely basic gospel requirement—the subject of Jesus' first sermon in Luke 4 and of his very last teaching to the disciples in Matthew 25. 31–46. But the cathedral must be engaged in this as an emblematic ministry that it holds alongside, and in prophetic tension with, its other overlapping roles.

At Derby Cathedral, the nave today becomes a night shelter once a week throughout winter. If that means worshippers sometimes have to put up with surprising consequences, that is all part of the learning, part of what it means to be a disciple. The Archer Project at Sheffield Cathedral[7] is probably the most extraordinary example in the Church of England of outreach to the poor, with a deeply established and much respected ministry among homeless people. Their strapline expresses beautifully how the project is experienced: "The thing about this place is they don't offer you help with A, B or C . . . They just offer to help." Another small city-centre cathedral with few resources offers a completely volunteer-led drop-in for homeless and marginalized people every Wednesday afternoon. Significantly, it normally takes place in one of the transepts, following straight on from the lunchtime Eucharist, as an explicit statement that this is simply what cathedrals do. This is where the Queen sat for a special service two years ago; this is where Colin, with his pit bull terrier, sits today. Another cathedral offers language classes for refugees. This project began in response to a very specific local need among a particular ethnic and linguistic group. Today it has over twenty-five nationalities across both volunteers and service users. In its first year the project grew so fast that it had to move from the space available in the cathedral to take over a whole floor in a nearby office block.

Cathedrals can be significant catalysts for change and partners in delivery. In one city, where begging has recently been made illegal, the cathedral through its partnerships and personnel has been involved in the provision and support of a night shelter, an Emmaus centre, a daytime drop-in, and a scheme (now adopted by the City Council and the city's commercial co-ordinating body) which enables people to donate, via boxes in shops, money that would otherwise have been given to beggars. This is then passed to the night shelter and other bodies for work with the homeless. The point again is that cathedrals exercise, or perhaps better, focus, a prophetic gospel ministry which—to have any serious credibility—must include a response to the core teaching of Jesus in the Beatitudes and elsewhere. It is not that this range of activities can only be done by cathedrals, but that it is emblematic that the cathedral does this precisely because it occupies public space in a unique way. So, in places where the *Magnificat* is sung daily, often very beautifully and at significant financial cost, it is foundational for cathedrals to respond to the mandate of this *Magnificat*. This is a calling for any kind of Christian community, but it is non-negotiable for a cathedral both because it is called to be exemplary and because this is how Christians learn to practise their faith, and, of course, because we are genuinely seeking to meet real human need. William Temple's great line (quoting Dick Sheppard) that the job of a Christian was to "see grandeur where it is least expected and sorrow where it is thought to be hidden"[8] should not be out of place in a cathedral's strategic plan. There is the shocking recognition, perhaps, that cathedrals are not measured by the splendour of their buildings or the glory of their worship, but by the quality of their love.

CONCLUSION

Stephen Cottrell, Bishop of Chelmsford and a former Canon Pastor of Peterborough Cathedral, sought to answer the question "What is a Cathedral for?" in this way:

> A cathedral is only a cathedral because a *cathedra* is in there. It is not just a big building, or an old building or a beautiful building, but the building which is the seat of the Bishop's ministry. Therefore what is a cathedral for? It is for the ministry of the Bishop. However, one of the ways we might helpfully understand and interpret this today is to see the Cathedral as the place where the episcopal and apostolic ministry is held, expounded and developed. Therefore if episcopal ministry is about oversight, teaching, pastoral care and evangelism (I have always understood a Bishop to be chief pastor and chief evangelist) then the ministry of the Cathedral should embody and exemplify this for the whole diocese.
>
> It is a place which is for the proclamation of the gospel; for the teaching of the gospel; for the care and welfare of the people of God, and especially clergy and other licensed ministers; and for the gathering together and good governance of the diocese. These four seem to me to be what a cathedral is about, though I can't help but notice I haven't mentioned worship in that list.

Of course all this is imbued with prayer and worship, but paradoxically worship does not make it onto my particular list of what the cathedral is for, whereas in the popular imagination I imagine that many people think first of the English choral tradition and all that lovely worship and think that's why cathedrals exist. The worship is primary to the ministry of every church, but is perhaps secondary—or at least a given—for that church which contains the Bishop's *cathedra*. The primary purpose for this church must be proclamation, catechesis, pastoral care and that other mix of ministries which I can't quite think of a word for which is about gathering, hospitality, oversight and governance.[9]

Several days a week, a man comes into the cathedral just after Evensong has begun and leaves just before it ends. During the worship he sits in silence, almost hidden in a small chapel at the far west end. No one knows his name, but somehow the building, the space, the liturgy unfolding provide a substructure to his day. A leader from the local Pentecostal community hears a call to establish 24–7 prayer across the city—and realizes the cathedral has to be at the heart of this. Here is a powerful intuitive recognition by someone to whom a cathedral might be alien, of precisely what it is really for. These are two small examples of how people access the spiritual and worshipping life of cathedrals very much on their own terms. They are examples that could be replicated at least forty-two times over. Bishop Stephen suggests, however, that this is not a cathedral's USP. Certainly prayer and worship are the foundation of everything, and in a cathedral the daily prayer has a particular significance and weight. But that is common, generic. "The worship is primary to the ministry of the church". Cathedrals are not agitating from the sidelines or making inappropriate claims about their importance or capacity. They can provide some of the necessary critical engagement and prophetic complementarity which can better allow the Church to be the Church, and to rediscover its apostolicity in active, outward-facing mission.

NOTES

1. "[S]eat of the bishop and a centre of worship and mission": this is from the opening section of the General Provisions of the Cathedrals Measure 1999: "Any person or body on whom functions are conferred by or under this Measure shall, in exercising those functions, have due regard to the fact that the cathedral is the seat of the bishop and a centre of worship and mission." It is also the minimum description of the role of a cathedral used by the Association of English Cathedrals and is included in the Constitution of every cathedral. Cf. also *Heritage and Renewal: The Report of the Archbishops' Commission on Cathedrals* (Church House Publishing, 1994).

2. Nine Old Foundation Cathedrals; thirteen New Foundation Cathedrals founded or re-founded by Henry VIII; nineteen cathedrals created from parish churches since 1836, and Liverpool and Guildford which were created as cathedrals without parishes.

3. The Cathedrals Measure 1999 creates a "body corporate" consisting of the Council, the Chapter, and the College of Canons. In effect the Chapter is the governing body and the Council and the College of Canons are supplementary bodies of non-executive directors with ill-defined powers and responsibilities.

4. "From Anecdote to Evidence: Findings from the Church Growth Research Programme 2011–2013" (Archbishops' Council, 2014), a report that set out to examine why growing churches were growing, across Parish Churches, Fresh Expressions of Church, Church Plants, and Cathedrals and Greater Churches.

5. Andrew Brown and Linda Woodhead, *That Was The Church That Was: How the Church of England Lost the English People* (Bloomsbury, 2016).

6. Over the last seventy years there has been a remarkable flowering of monastic communities in France, just as the life of parish churches has increasingly felt exhausted. The ecumenical community at Taizé is the most famous, but the Jerusalem Community is another outstanding example, with increasing presence in other European countries (<http://jerusalem.cef.fr/jerusalem/en/en_21tous.html>). There are many more local examples.

7. For the Archer Project, see their website (<http://www.archerproject.org.uk>).

8. H. R. L. Sheppard, in *The Human Parson* (Murray, 1924), wrote of love in its highest manifestation, "It sees sorrow where sorrow is thought to be hidden, and virtue and grandeur where it is least expected."

9.   Email to the Dean of Chelmsford, 4 April 2014, in response to the "Dean's
     Big Question: what is Chelmsford Cathedral for?"

10. THE PLACE OF ART
IN CATHEDRALS

Christopher Irvine

CATHEDRAL OR GALLERY?

The pedestrian Millennium Bridge, strung across the River Thames, links Tate Modern and St Paul's Cathedral, two institutions that might appear to compete, the art gallery and the cathedral. Around 60 per cent of photos of the bridge on Google images show St Paul's Cathedral, but it is the art that draws people, and it is Tate Modern that has the larger footfall with five million visitors a year, and an enviable demographic with an estimated 50 per cent of visitors being under the age of thirty-five. One wonders if Tate Modern has now become the kind of "public space" that Christopher Wren envisaged for his cathedral, built, incidentally, by public subscription to be the sacred space in the City of London for the people of London. The Gallery certainly wants to provide space for the public as well as its art, just as the Cathedral wants to make provision for its visitors as well as its worshippers. As an architectural commentator has said, comparisons are inevitably drawn,[1] and to this I would add that comparisons may be too *easily* drawn.

In a BBC television documentary on the recently opened extension of Tate Modern, the Switch House (now known as the Blavatnik Building), built at the cost of over 250 million pounds, Andrew Marr almost stretched the comparison to breaking point.[2] He not only spoke of the gallery as a "secular cathedral" but also referred to its visitors as the "flock" and the "art congregation", but surely this is more the language of ironic parody than the drawing of a suggestive analogy?

The architecture and the art of the gallery and the cathedral arguably raise our sights, inviting us to look with care and not simply to see what meets the eye, and the curators of both kinds of institutions occasionally make lofty claims about the power of art to raise important questions of who and what we are. This may be true in some cases, but in the art world the artist often caps the art, and the viewer wants to see a Louise Bourgeois, or a Rachel Whiteread, rather than engaging with the artwork itself. Some contemporary work is serious, and some, like the kind of interactive art in the Switch House, is playful. But this does not equate simply with the "wondrous playfulness of the liturgy"[3] for which a cathedral is built. Meanwhile the gallery, too, has its own specific institutional function.

It is interesting to note, for example, that in discussions about what it is that makes modern art, the very fact that it is placed in a gallery is a sufficient qualification for an artwork or installation to be deemed art.[4] Both the cathedral and the gallery have their particular roles to play and comparisons, of course, can work in both directions. For if museums and galleries are the new cathedrals, then it could be that the need to increase visitor numbers and benefit from the heritage economy is leading some to regard cathedrals as the new museums and galleries.

As I have argued elsewhere,[5] the broader question of what we *see* when we view a piece of art will depend to some extent on *where* it is seen and the occasion on which it is seen. And what comes into play here is not simply the setting in which art is sited, where it is placed, but the other objects that will come into the viewer's field of vision as they look at a painting or other work of art. Placed in a cathedral, an artwork is sited in a densely symbolically-charged environment, whereas the art gallery arguably provides the best conditions for exhibiting and viewing art, with its capacious and uncluttered white spaces, bespoke lighting, and environmental controls. Of course art can be viewed as art in a cathedral setting, but it is interesting to reflect on the differences between viewing a work in a gallery and in the setting for which it was commissioned. Canterbury Cathedral loaned the Winifred Knights altarpiece, *The Life of St Martin* (c. 1928–33), to an exhibition of Knights' work at the Dulwich

Picture Gallery in the summer of 2016. The exhibition was superbly curated, and it was interesting to view a familiar painting in a gallery setting. It was certainly instructive to see the painting in relation to the narrative of the artist, but what was particularly striking was not simply seeing, but noticing some of the detail of the painting for the first time in the conditions of the gallery. There the viewer saw more, and yet the painting had been deliberately commissioned for, and certainly works as, part of the ensemble of St Martin's Chapel in the north-east transept of the cathedral.

There is much more that could be said here in comparing galleries to cathedrals and cathedrals to museums, but suffice to say that there is nothing intrinsically wrong in seeing the one in terms of the other. It is really a matter of seeking a greater clarity about how we place art in cathedrals and why. The issues are more nuanced, and cathedral chapters (and possibly councils too) should give time to discuss what it means to see galleries as cathedrals and cathedrals as museums, particularly as they relate to the cathedral's mission statement and the role of a cathedral, as it is defined in the Cathedrals Measure (1999), to be a centre of worship and mission. And as such, cathedrals should help the visitor see the religious import or significance of a work of art in the cathedral through signage, interpretive notes, and printed and audio guides. As Janet Martin Soskice commented some years ago, churches often provide art-historical notes, but fail to assist the visitor to see the religious significance of what it is that they may be looking at.[6]

SEEING IN CONTEXT

There are different "ways of seeing" and some of these ways will require specific conditions in terms of the setting. Some might ask, for instance, whether contemporary art actually works in a cathedral setting. The often sterile conditions of the contemporary gallery, even the new white spaces in Tate Modern's Switch Room, help to focus the viewer's attention on the art. In a cathedral, whether it is a mediaeval building or a modern cathedral like Coventry, filled with what was considered to be the very best of modern art by Graham Sutherland, John Piper, and Elizabeth Frink, the art and architecture are intentionally and artfully combined as an ensemble to serve the primary purpose of the building. A cathedral, unlike the art gallery, is not, as Jonathan Koestlé-Cate says, a blank canvas.[7] But this is neither a counsel of despair, nor a statement that the role of art in a cathedral is simply to serve the liturgy, but an observation that contemporary art in a cathedral has to compete with a plethora of visual stimuli: the glass, the architectural features, monuments, paintings, and sculpture, as well as the liturgical furniture and furnishings. Nevertheless, there are examples of contemporary art in the spaces of a cathedral that work, and work extremely well, in opening up significant questions.

Anthony Gormley's "Transport" in the eastern crypt of Canterbury Cathedral is a good example. Though contemporary, this sculpture is site-specific in that it is fabricated with mediaeval nails retrieved when the south-east transept was being re-roofed, and is suspended over the site where Thomas Becket was buried following his brutal murder in 1174. The resonance in this historical setting is finely tuned, and the body-shaped work, open to the air and light, captures the gaze of visitors and pilgrims alike, and raises the question of what it is to be a person, a psychosomatic unity of body, mind, and spirit.

Another notable example of contemporary art in a cathedral context is Bill Viola's permanent four-panelled video installation "Martyrs (Earth, Air, Fire, Water)" in the eastern termination of the south aisle of St Paul's Cathedral. Much has been made of the ubiquity of this digital medium and of how it attracts and engages contemporary audiences. But this is not without ambiguity, for the medium itself may well illustrate the fluidity and iconoclasm of contemporary culture, and amplify the question of how we can witness to the stability of transcendent truth in an increasingly unsafe, insecure, and uncertain world. The deliberate time lapses and slow motion of the images in this work, however, effectively hold the viewer's attention; whether this seven-minute film succeeds in raising the question as to what one might actually die for is an open question. This is far from safe art. Perhaps by seeing these disturbing flickering images in this setting rather than in a darkened installation space in a gallery, the viewer is more able to face a world that is bent on self-destruction.

Moreover, having viewed the video in this setting, the visitor can turn and then see other signs of life through death in this light-filled space.

If we return to the Millennium Bridge and walk south over the Thames we will see the letters on the façade of the Tate Modern building which spell out the message, "Art changes. We change." Here is a deliberate play on words. With theological propriety we could easily substitute the word "worship" for "art" as we reflect on cathedrals as centres of mission and worship. Worship too changes, and it can change lives. For when worshippers attentively place themselves with open hearts and minds before the triune God, they can be changed into the likeness of Christ, themselves becoming the living art of God. Worship changes, and worship can indeed change our lives.[8]

So although there may well be tensions, and even contradictory aims, between the art world and the world of the Church, as represented by a cathedral, there is an extraordinary correspondence and overlap between the aims of the liturgist and the maker of art. Here I use the word "liturgist" in the widest sense of the word as those who give themselves to be formed by worship. This touches the very core activity of the corporate vocation of the Church, perhaps seen in its most concentrated form in the life of a religious community. Many of our great cathedrals, of course, were originally monastic foundations, and although the cathedral today has to play many different roles, looking to our monastic roots recalls us to our primary corporate vocation, that is, to be a praying community.

The term vocation has a strong religious connotation and is less often applied to the artist.[9] And yet, in the stories of many artists there is a recognition of an inner compulsion to make art, a sense that the artists' identity, of who they are, is bound up in the very making of art.

A poignant example is the elusive poet, calligrapher, and artist David Jones (1895–1974). Like most of his generation, Jones felt compelled to enrol in the army in 1915, despite his poor physique and his sensitive temperament. As a soldier in the (London) Welsh Fusiliers, Jones was deployed in the Battle of the Somme and was seriously wounded below Mametz Wood. The clinging mud, the constant bombardment, and the wasteland of the battlefield took their toll, but through it all, Jones was sustained by an inexplicable feeling that he would survive because of his call, his vocation to be an artist.[10] The confluence of religious and artistic sensibility is illustrated by the story that on one occasion, while on an evening foray to gather wood for a fire, Jones came across a celebration of the Mass in a dilapidated barn with a couple of empty ammunition cases as an altar. Jones' gaze was held by what struck him as the simple beauty of the ritual action of Communion. He later sketched the scene, and alluded to this numinous sight in his novel-length poem "In Parenthesis", a poem that is regarded as one of the most realistic depictions of the First World War. Here the vocation of the artist, captivated and drawn by a vision of the beauty of the transcendent Otherness, corresponds to that of the worshipper who is brought to the very edge of language when they cry, "Holy, holy, holy."

THE ART OF WORSHIP

As illustrated by the scene stumbled upon by David Jones, it may not be necessary for art to be placed where we worship, but a sufficient understanding of liturgy will recognize that worship itself is "artful". Significant differences may indeed exist between the mission and life of the Church and an art world driven by celebrity and corporate culture, resulting in the absurdly inflated prices of the art market. Nevertheless, there are parallels to be drawn between the making and showing of art and the performance of worship. Space prohibits a full exploration, but let me make four indicative points in summary form to illustrate how these two areas of art and worship may overlap, illuminate, and interpret each other.

1. The liturgical theologian Odo Casel (1886–1948), from the Rhineland Abbey of Maria Laach, a major centre of the twentieth-century continental Liturgical Movement, regarded liturgy as being a synthesis of the arts. For in addition to the art and architecture of its setting, worship draws together a whole symphony of the arts, including music and song, performance of biblical texts, the poetry of prayer, ritual movement, as well as the use of festal garments worn by the ministers during the celebration of the liturgy. This whole

panoply corresponds to Richard Wagner's description of opera as a total work of art, of what he called a *Gesamtkunstwerk*,[11] insofar as it brought together various artistic forms and media, including music, libretto, movement, and the visual arts of costume and the stage scenery. On the basis of this correspondence, worship too can be seen as a form of art.

2. It could be argued that both the artist and the liturgist (as defined above) are what a Dominican theologian once described as being a "seeker of form". This expression was appropriated by David Jones, who applied it to his account of the sacramental expression of Christ's presence.[12] This language of form occurs in the writing of his contemporary, the art critic Clive Bell. According to Bell, what the painter and the sculptor endeavoured to do was to discern and reveal "significant form".[13] The revealing of "significant form" may also be construed as the intended outcome of worship as the art of God, the showing and repristination of that *imago Dei* in which all human beings are made.

3. The making of art and the offering of worship may both be viewed as "doxology", that is, the expression of praise for the sheer gratuity and excess of creation. Praise is both a response to the wonder that anything should exist at all, and the irrepressible expression of human creativity. Many artists hint at this aspect of "making" as a celebration of what there is, especially those who work with the materials that are at hand. The sense of making as praise was explicitly articulated by the sculptor Barbara Hepworth, who once claimed that every true work of art was an act of praise. In this sense, the shaping and making of art could be seen as being analogous to what is expressed in many liturgical texts such as the *Benedicite* or St Francis of Assisi's Canticle of Creation. The artistic and the liturgical converge superbly in the exuberant lines, vibrant colours, and figures of Marc Chagall's stained-glass window in Chichester Cathedral, commissioned by Walter Hussey. This window, which was called "Let everything that has breath", was inspired by the verse in Psalm 150 which suggests that the gift of creation, the inbreathing of God's breath, is repaid by the expression of praise: "Let everything that has breath, praise the Lord."(Psalm 150. 6)

4. A further correspondence between art and worship may be seen in that both are dialogical. In different and various ways they both call us into a conversation and demand a response. Worship is indivisible from the *missio Dei*, and that is why it invites our attentive participation and response. The sculptor Naum Gabo expressed the view in a letter to the critic Herbert Read that a work of art was incomplete until it was seen and responded to by a viewer. Both art and worship require our attentive engagement and response.

Many other analogies may suggest themselves, but perhaps what is sketched out here is sufficient to convince us that worship too is an art-form, and therefore ought to be planned and performed with the same kind of care that a curator shows in staging an art exhibition, and that art certainly has a place in the setting of worship.

Needless to say, cathedrals are intricate works of art in themselves. These complex buildings are truly iconic, and many also bear the marks of the iconoclasm of the Reformation and the English Civil War. Examples of the art might include the sculpted stone façade of Wells Cathedral, the painted roof bosses in the nave at Norwich, carved wooden misericords, as well as paintings and stained glass, and, for the scars of iconoclasm, we can recall the example of the Lady Chapel at Ely Cathedral. The great symphony of art in our cathedrals conspires to make the invisible visible, to signal the transcendent, to celebrate human skill and creativity, and in lofty elevations and soaring architectural lines to give visible expression of the Christian hope of the heavenly Jerusalem. Cathedral churches are found in a variety of architectural styles, but what distinguishes them all is the scale of the building, and the primary purpose for which they were built, namely worship. Our great Romanesque and Gothic cathedrals were built to resound with the voice of prayer and praise as the sound rolls around vaulted ceilings. The *opus Dei* was, and in most places still is, sung, and it is the sound of this "singing of the Word"[14] that completes the architecture. Indeed, the spaces of the quire, chancel, and nave are exceptional acoustical spaces, and were originally built for processional singing and the chanting of psalms and canticles.

In his lyrical reflections on French cathedrals, the sculptor Auguste Rodin noted how these monumental buildings came alive when voices were raised in song and music was made in them.[15] A contemporary art project that combined sight and sound was Sophie Hacker's "Messiaen Project". The artist had made nine abstract "icons of the incarnation", each with striking forms and vibrant colour, inspired by the nine movements of Olivier Messiaen's organ suite *La Nativité du Seigneur*. The project was taken to seven English cathedrals, including Winchester, Chichester, and Canterbury in 2009, and was a multi-media event. At Canterbury, during the Epiphany season, the artwork was exhibited in the Chapter House, and on one evening an audience had the opportunity to view the art at a reception before moving to the Quire for a performance of the organ suite. As the suite was being played, a film projected the matching art onto a large screen set up in front of the high altar. By the combination of both sight and sound, the audience was brought to contemplate the mystery before which, as one Byzantine defender of icons claimed, all language fails. Cathedrals, in short, should not only be places where music resounds, but also places of striking visual art too.

EXHIBITIONS

Most cathedrals appear now to be inundated with requests from artists and arts organisations to hold exhibitions somewhere in the building. Having an exhibition in a cathedral certainly gives the artist kudos and, understandably, cathedrals want to be seen as being both welcoming and socially engaged. But perhaps a more discerning approach should be careful to avoid simply capitalizing on the resurgence of interest in the visual arts. And so cathedrals are increasingly selective, setting out criteria for exhibitions and drawing up professional exhibition agreements for the artists/organisers and the cathedral. The aims, terms and conditions, including insurance and invigilation arrangements, are clearly set out and agreed. In the preamble to its guidelines issued to those enquiring about exhibitions, one cathedral expresses its intention to become more proactive in the process. Another cathedral stipulates that artwork will only be accepted for exhibition if it relates to the articulated statement of the cathedral's life and mission. In this case, the example given is that of art which would directly enhance the cathedral's educational engagement with children and young people.

This may sound rather restrictive, but is it simply a matter of managing the increasing demand on the organizational capacities of cathedrals? It is perfectly legitimate to ask why and for what purpose art is being brought in to be exhibited in a cathedral space. It is all too easy to see transepts and chapter houses simply as exhibition spaces. Critical questions should be asked, but above all, more dialogue is required between cathedral chapters and those seeking to exhibit their work within the transcendental spaces of a cathedral. Dialogue is, however, a two-way process, and one that takes time. There is a need to address both curatorial and theological questions about how the art will function in the proposed space, and how it might be received and responded to there, rather than in a gallery. The practical need to manage events and the desire for better dialogue both suggest that it may be better if there were fewer art exhibitions in cathedrals. Those exhibitions that are hosted by cathedrals need to be better curated, and the multivalent significance of the space in which the exhibition takes place should be recognized by all the parties involved.

In addition to exhibitions, there are other ways in which cathedrals may engage with artists and the wider community. Having an artist-in-residence, for example, gives both parties greater opportunities for shared conversation, the kind of conversation that may yield new and possibly surprising insights about the particular spaces in and around the cathedral.

A recent project at Birmingham Cathedral is a notable example of another kind of engagement. Over a substantial period of time, the cathedral worked with an artistic director on a community arts project that was integral to its three hundredth anniversary celebrations. Real benefits in terms of mutual shared learning and discovery, social cohesion, and creativity have evidently accrued from this project.[16] Unfortunately, there are other examples of art being brought into cathedrals which have had a minimal significance in terms of social engagement and, indeed, in promoting the cathedral's mission.

There is more that can and should be said about the placing of art in cathedrals, but let us be clear about what is *not* being said here. First, I am not saying that the art brought into cathedrals should be restricted to liturgical art, or to art that depicts a conventional religious subject. The function of art in these sacred spaces is not simply to serve the liturgy as, for example, liturgical furnishings and furniture should, but rather to be in conversation with an aspect of all that comes to expression in a liturgical celebration. But whether exhibited in or around the cathedral, there should be an answer to the question, "Why is *this* piece being exhibited *here*?" The choice should not be arbitrary. In deciding what to exhibit where, the decision should be made on whether the artwork has a resonance with the space in which it is to be displayed. At its best, art should assist us in our apprehension and re-apprehension of the divine mystery played out in the performance of worship. The mystery of God that is played out is partially disclosed and partly hidden, shown and concealed in what is often experienced as a puzzling, disturbing, and uncertain world. Let me try to explore what is implied about the kind of art that is required for this to occur, in terms of the installation and commissioning of artwork for a cathedral church.

TEMPORARY AND PERMANENT INSTALLATIONS

There are important distinctions to be made between temporary and permanent installations of art in a cathedral and its precincts. Both require fairly stringent criteria, not to censor the art, but to discern how the artwork may work in the proposed setting. The installation of art should never be a vanity project, a means to increase the footfall of visitors, or to secure media attention, but a way of capturing the attention of visitors and worshippers alike. Instead, we want the viewers not simply to see the artwork, but really to *look*, and then to look and look more deeply and honestly at themselves, at our world, and at how that world may be re-imagined. This is not to say that the artwork will give us the answers, but it can open questions about who we are as people, of how our world is, and what God's final purpose might be. Good art invites and even challenges the viewer to attend more deeply, and to reflect on what is really real. For this to happen, a cathedral would want to install artwork that is visually striking, and engaging.

As a basic rule of thumb, a temporary artwork should be installed for a limited time and should relate in some way to what is being celebrated, whether that is a local arts festival, a liturgical feast day, or a season of the Christian year. The artwork may be topical, or may assist the viewer to focus on the mood or theme of the particular time or season. The artwork should add to, rather than detract from, the wider "message" that the cathedral community wishes to convey to both visitors and worshippers. The annual Lenten exhibition of artwork at Southwark Cathedral often achieves this.

The installation of permanent works of art requires an even greater scrutiny, and among the range of considerations I would cluster the following key issues:

First, very careful consideration needs to be given to how a newly commissioned work of art will fit the architectural setting in which it is to be placed. The new can exist with the old, the abstract with the figurative, right angles with curves, and so the artwork introduced into the space does not necessarily need to be all of a piece and form a harmonious whole. Indeed, a cathedral is often a palimpsest, a historically and stylistically layered building, displaying a variety of often contrasting styles. The point here is that each element, both separately, and in relation to other elements and to their setting, should combine in serving to articulate the significance of a sacred, public space.

Second, permanent art installed in a cathedral should be durable rather than ephemeral. It should be fabricated from authentic and good quality materials. It should be sufficiently strong in its design not only to capture the attention of the viewer, but also to support the articulated aims of a community that seeks God and seeks to promote community with others in a fractured world. In itself, the artwork should have the qualities to intrigue, to delight, to puzzle, and to inspire the viewer, though obviously not simultaneously or in equal measure.

COMMISSIONING NEW ART

There are a whole range of considerations that touch on the practicalities of placing art in a cathedral setting. The first, already mentioned, is the question about who should be involved in the various stages of the process. This may begin with the handling of a gift or legacy given for the express purpose of securing a significant piece of art for a cathedral. Then it will include the selection of an artist, the establishing of a search committee, the possible engagement of an art consultant, the framing of advice to be sought from the cathedral's Fabric Advisory Committee and, if necessary, from the Cathedrals Fabric Commission for England.

It is certainly expedient for the chapter to work with a visual art consultant. In that discussion there are a number of preliminary questions that will need to be addressed in drawing up a brief for an artist. Among them I would suggest the following:

5. First, there needs to be clarity about the kind of artwork that is going to be commissioned. Consideration must be given to where it is to be located and how it may fit and enhance that part of the building.

6. Whether installing a new window, a sculpture, or even digital media, the different uses of the space need to be carefully mapped, and specific questions asked about how the artwork might relate to all that happens in that space.

7. In relation to this mapping of the space, questions should be asked about whether the proposed artwork will detract from, or expand, enlarge, and even challenge our understandings of what is expressed liturgically in our acts of worship.

8. Another set of questions relating to the siting of the work is more curatorial. These questions range from how the art work sits within its architectural setting to how the intended piece relates to the other art work that is placed in the same location. When new glass for a window is being designed and made, for instance, consideration should be given to how it may relate to the windows and architectural features on either side of its proposed location in the building.

9. The final question focuses on the aesthetic significance and impact
    of the new work. Reflecting on the purpose of a church building,
    the protagonist in Peter Carey's novel *Oscar and Lucinda* says that
    ultimately the purpose of the building is to *celebrate* God,[17] and
    perhaps this could also be extended and applied to the artwork
    that is installed in the building. Does it puzzle, suggest questions,
    or awaken a sense of the mystery in which human beings live and
    move and have their being?

A work of art can function in different ways, and may be seen and
experienced in various and often undetermined ways. And yet, as Frank
Burch Brown suggests, good religious art should achieve one or more of
the following: it should illuminate life and glorify God, invite us to explore
sin and suffering, release the joy of being alive, unsettle and soothe, and
invite us to be still.[18]

Gauging and predicting the impact and reception of art is an inexact
science, and how viewers respond to a work depends to some extent
on where, by whom, and on what occasion the art is seen.[19] When the
work is installed, an opportunity should be given for the new work to
be received and welcomed by the worshipping community. The artist
should be present on this occasion when the art work is "unveiled" and
dedicated to the God who we believe takes, re-makes, and redeems the
material of the created world.

THE FUTURE OF ART IN CATHEDRALS

In recent years the Cathedrals Fabric Commission for England (CFCE),
the statutory planning body for work on cathedrals and their precincts,
has encouraged cathedral chapters to write an arts policy to set out
their thinking about the place of art in the cathedral, and to detail the
commissioning process. Approval has to be given by the CFCE for
the installation of any permanent art work in a cathedral, and for the
installation of any temporary piece that would have a material effect on

the fabric of the building.[20] Advice on these matters should also be sought from the cathedral's Fabric Advisory Committee as a matter of course. It is interesting to note that in the guidance note posted on the ChurchCare website, the criteria published by the CFCE include the "visual impact" of the proposed new art on the character and appreciation of the building as a whole. Implicit here is a concern to safeguard the integrity of the architectural lines of the cathedral. The understanding is that a cathedral's arts policy is a living document and that it will be periodically revised and updated. This is certainly exemplified by Norwich Cathedral in a whole raft of recent documentation, including a four-page exhibitions policy and exhibition application form. Norwich Cathedral, like Winchester, has evidently benefitted considerably from the advice of experts and art consultants.

In the course of his research on contemporary art and the Church, Jonathan Koestlé-Cate has scrutinized a range of cathedral arts policies. He evidently welcomes the increasing engagement of the Church with the visual arts, but sees a rather cautious and, in some instances, restrictive approach to contemporary art in these policies.[21] However, these policies should be seen more as guidelines than as strict regulations, and their aim should be to provide a framework to facilitate the kind of mutual dialogue that respects and trusts the artist, and which enables an informed appreciation of the context in which the art may be installed. For their part, cathedral chapters do need to achieve a greater clarity and consistency both in their criteria for the installation and commissioning of new art, and in setting the conditions for exhibitions of art in and around the cathedral. Some of the language used in these documents will inevitably be elusive and suggestive. But all this simply underlines the need for a more searching dialogue between the members of a cathedral chapter and the artist, and for the artist herself to have more of a voice both in shaping the concept of the proposed work and in discussions about where and how the work may be placed in the building. This can be achieved when there is real dialogue.

A good example of a three-way dialogue between cathedral, theologian, and artist is well documented as part of the Theology Through the Arts project.[22] Theological reflection is to be commended, as is an informed appreciation of how a cathedral building is used liturgically, and in this regard it is good to see that the CFCE guidelines for an application for the installation of a new art work require a reference to the cathedral's liturgical plan in the application. The questions can, of course, come from both directions, not only the question of how an art work may fit into a liturgical space, but also the question of how the proposed art may influence how the liturgy will be celebrated in the particular space in which it is installed.

A model of engagement with artists is currently demonstrated by a community that is centred on the liturgy, the Community of the Resurrection at Mirfield. Despite limited financial resources, an artist-in-residence scheme is well established, and new work has been commissioned from Nicholas Mynheer and Mark Cazalet for the recently re-ordered church that is of the scale of a small cathedral. Mynheer has produced striking panels for an altar sculpted with scenes of resurrection appearances, and Cazalet has installed etched and engraved glass screens depicting scenes from the story of Mary Magdalene for the Reconciliation Chapel. A number of cathedrals could also be commended, Liverpool among them, but perhaps Durham Cathedral deserves mention for consistently commissioning quality art by artists with strong local and international connections.[23] Recent commissions have included Fenwick Lawson's wondrously expressive wooden sculpture, "Pieta" (1981), a figurative picture (pastel on paper) by Paula Rego, "Margaret and David" (2003), in her distinctive and not universally appreciated style, and a window designed by the master glass-maker Tom Denny, "Transfiguration", a celebration in colour, light, and delicate draughtsmanship, installed in 2010 to commemorate Archbishop Michael Ramsey's association with the city and its cathedral.

Quality commissions such as these are to be celebrated, especially those which in the process foster the kind of dialogue that utilizes a variety of languages, discourses, and technologies.[24] Art has a place in cathedrals. We may not need more and more art, but we do want good art and a better shared understanding of why art has a place in these great buildings. In an increasingly brutal, violent, and uncertain world, we need our cathedrals to be places not only of welcome and safety, but also of re-enchantment and hope, where all those who cross the threshold may catch a glimpse of the transforming beauty of God.

NOTES

1. See Philip Jodidio (ed.), *Architecture Now! Museums* (Taschen, 2010), p. 8.

2. Screened on BBC 2, at 20.00 on Saturday 18 June 2016.

3. See Romano Guardini, *The Spirit of the Liturgy* (Sheed and Ward, 1930), pp. 85–129.

4. The very placing of a work in a gallery brings that work into an institutional and a conceptual space in which the viewer may see and respond to it as a work of art. See Daniel A. Siedell, *God in the Gallery: A Christian Embrace of Modern Art* (Baker Academic Press, 2008), especially pp. 24–26.

5. Christopher Irvine, *The Cross and Creation in Christian Liturgy and Art* (SPCK, 2013), Chapter 1, "Liturgical Seeing".

6. Janet Martin Soskice, "Churches must help tourists to see as well as to look", *The Times*, 26 May 2001.

7. Jonathan Koestlé-Cate, *Art and the Church: A Fractious Embrace: Ecclesiastical Encounters with Contemporary Art* (Routledge, 2016).

8. I attempted to chart how the aim and intent of worship is the formation of the worshipper in the likeness of Christ in *The Art of God: The Making of Christians and the Meaning of Worship* (SPCK, 2005).

9. The role of the artist in different epochs and cultural contexts in terms of vocation is set out in a fascinating study by Deborah J. Haynes, *The Vocation of the Artist* (Cambridge University Press, 1997).

10. See Keith Alldritt, *David Jones: Writer and Artist* (Constable, 2003), Chapter 3, and Ariane Bankes and Paul Hills, *The Art of David Jones: Vision and Memory* (Lund Humphries, 2015).

11. For an account of the drama of liturgy see George Guiver CR's *Vision upon Vision: Processes of Change and Renewal in Christian Worship* (Canterbury Press, 2009), pp. 32–33, and Chapter 3.

12. See David Jones, "Art and Sacrament", in *Epoch and Artist* (Faber and Faber, 1959).

13. Clive Bell, *Art* (Chatto and Windus, 1914).

14. I am indebted to Peter Allan CR for this telling expression.

15. Auguste Rodin, trans. Elisabeth Chase Geissbuhler, *Cathedrals of France* (Beacon Press, 1965).

16. An interview between the Dean and the Artistic Director is in *Art and Christianity* 86, Summer 2016, pp. 16–18.

17. Peter Carey, *Oscar and Lucinda* (Queensland University Press, 1988).

18. Frank Burch Brown, *Inclusive Yet Discerning: Navigating Worship Artfully* (William B. Eerdmans, 2009), pp. 86–87.

19. Irvine, *The Cross and Creation*, Chapter 1.

20. ChurchCare's guidance notes (<http://www.churchcare.co.uk/images/Cathedrals_Guidance_Note_New_Art_FINAL.pdf>) were shaped by working closely with Art and Christianity Enquiry (ACE), and by two recent conferences, one at Sarum College in 2009, and another, the following year, at Durham, built on Tom Devonshire Jones and Graham Howes' work, *English Cathedrals and the Visual Arts: Patronage, Policies and Provision 2005* (ACE, 2005).

21. Koestlé-Cate, *Art and the Church*, pp. 198–9.

22. See Alastair McFadyen and John Inge, "Art in a Cathedral", and Vanessa Herrick, "Interview with Jonathan Clarke", in Jeremy Begbie (ed.), *Sounding the Depths: Theology Through the Arts* (SCM Press, 2002), Chapters 11 and 12.

23. See John Munns, "Twentieth Century Art Works", in David Brown (ed.), *Durham Cathedral: History, Fabric and Culture* (Yale University Press, 2015).

24. See Julia Porter-Pryce, "A critical context" in *Art and Christianity* 86, Summer 2016, pp. 2–5.

GENERAL INDEX

INDEX OF BIBLE REFERENCES